Visions of Modern Finnish Design

Visions of Modern Finnish Design

Edited by Anne Stenros

Otava Publishing Company Ltd.

Published in cooperation with The Finnish Society of Crafts and Design

Authors:
Carla Enbom
Pekka Korvenmaa
Markku Norvasuo
Hannele Nyman
Tuula Poutasuo
Päikki Priha
Liisa Räsänen
Anne Stenros
Pekka Suhonen
Pekka Toivonen
Jukka Valtasaari
Anne Veinola
Ritva Wäre

Translation:
John Arnold and Jüri Kokkonen

Graphic design and layout:
Kalervo Katajavuori

Cover design:
Kalervo Katajavuori
Cover photograph:
Rauno Träskelin

Printed by:
Otava Book Printing Ltd.
Keuruu 1999

ISBN 951-1-16004-4

Carla Enbom, BA, freelance journalist and translator. Ms. Enbom has written extensively on design and applied arts for newspapers and magazines.

Pekka Korvenmaa, PhD, Docent in Art History and Research Director at the University of Art and Design Helsinki. Mr Korvenmaa is the author of numerous books and articles published in Finland and abroad on the history of Finnish architecture and applied arts.

Hannele Nyman, freelance author and researcher with the Arabia Museum, Helsinki.

Tuula Poutasuo, MA, is an art historian and a freelance journalist. Ms. Poutasuo has edited several books on design and the applied arts in addition to authoring a large number of articles on design for newspapers and periodicals.

Päikki Priha is a textile designer and Professor of Textile and Clothing Design at the University of Art and Design Helsinki.

Liisa Räsänen, until 1994 curator and researcher at the Department of General Studies of the University of Art and Design Helsinki. Ms. Räsänen has written a large number of articles on design and the applied arts.

Anne Stenros, Dr Sc. (Tech.), Docent in Architecture at the Helsinki University of Technology. Ms Stenros has been managing director of the Finnish Society of Crafts and Design/ Design Forum and editor-in-chief of the journal *Form Function Finland* since 1995.

Pekka Suhonen, author. Mr Suhonen has written articles and books on Tapio Wirkkala, Marimekko and Artek, as well as essays on modern architecture and antiquity, and works of fiction and poetry.

Pekka Toivanen is a designer and chairman of the TKO Industrial Designers Association of Finland.

Jukka Valtasaari, Lic. Pol.Sc., is Secretary of State at the Finnish Foreign Ministry. Mr Valtasaari was the Finnish Ambassador to Washington from 1988 until 1996.

Anne Veinola is an architect and a researcher in art history and aesthetics. She is also editor of *Form Function Finland*.

Riva Wäre, PhD and docent in Art History at the University of Helsinki. Ms Wäre has been the director of the National Museum of Finland since 1992.

Contents

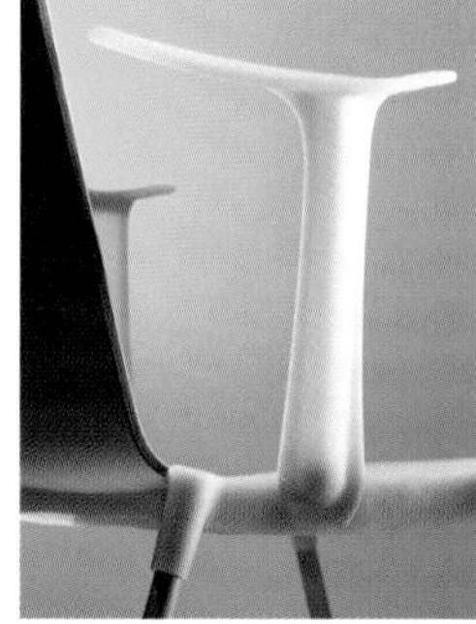

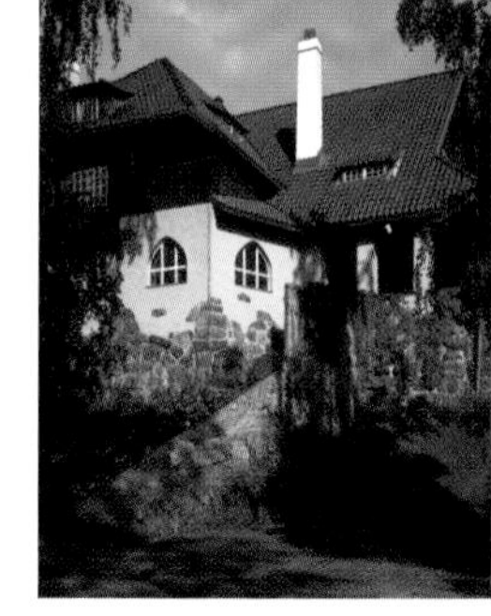

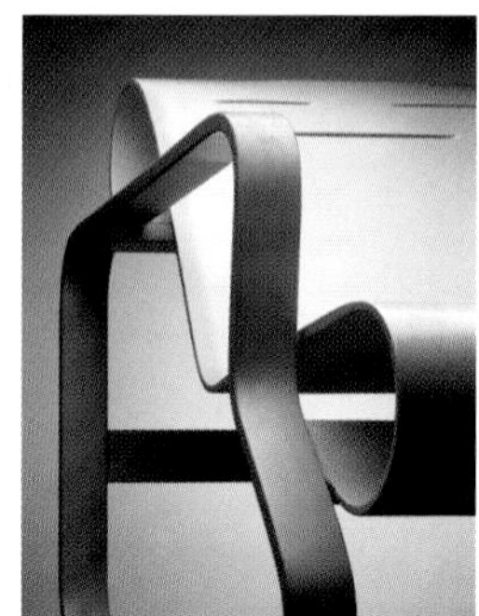

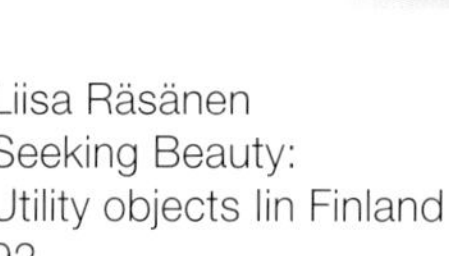

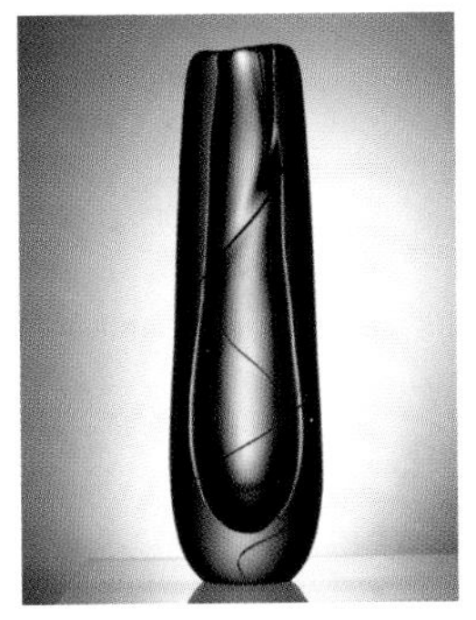

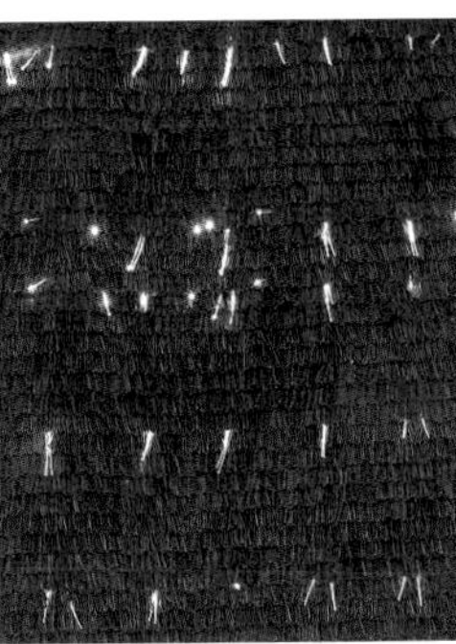

Quality and Insight: National Culture and Public Authority

Jukka Valtasaari

◀◀ *The Embassy of Finland in Washington, the roof and terrace. Photo Jussi Tiainen.*

▶ *The Embassy of Finland in Washington, the staircase and exibition hall. Architects Mikko Heikkinen and Markku Komonen, 1994.*

What will happen to national culture in a world characterized by internationalization, convergence and globalization? No doubt it will thrive, retaining its currency when expanded international contact adds sparkle to its substance. Culture lives on in our world of today, where borders have become meeting places if they have not entirely vanished. English has two words for the line between two countries: border and frontier. Here I am referring to the second of these. The world of the Internet, which has replaced hierarchies at meeting places, is making this way of thinking inevitable.

Another question is: is there anything new about this Euro-age? The noted French author and columnist Jean François Revel has the answer to this: "Cultural history is comprised of the recycling of ideas and their absorption. Only in this way is insight achieved."

In his 1992 article *L'ouverture aux Cultures Etrangères*, Revel mocked the overprotective attitude of the French towards their national culture. At that time, the entire liberalization of world trade seemed to be hostage to the French demand for quotas on foreign films shown by television in France. The "problem" was domination by American films – the same film industry whose leading names include Chaplin, von Stroheim, Lubitsch and Capra, as Revel pointed out.

Anne Stenros

The Classic Makers exhibition by Design Forum in the Embassy of Finland, 1997.

We Finns also have examples of how national culture is sparked by contact between cultures and people – starting from the Kalevala, our national epic. In the golden age of Finnish painting at the turn of the twentieth century, many Finnish artists found their way to a nationally meaningful expression of national sentiment by way of Paris, with Gallen-Kallela in the forefront.

The subject of public authority, the second half of my heading, tempts me to assert that without national culture there might be no public authority. After all, culture played a pivotal role in the evolution of Finland in the 19th century from a nation into a nation-state. In the troubled years at the beginning of the 20th century, artists from different fields – Saarinen, Sibelius and Leino – unitedly clothed their national statements in architecture, music and poetry. The importance of an existing body of culture to the first years of independence is understood better now that it can be compared to the struggle for independence of countries which lacked the heritage of a century of cultural incubation. A flag and coat of arms are essential but inadequate implements with which to set out on the road to becoming a nation-state.

In weighing the relationship between national culture and public authority, the time, place, world-view and culture are major factors. In the USA, these are largely separated. The National Museum, the National Art Foundation, National Public Radio and certain other institutions have regular access to the public purse, but a substantial proportion of the funds used for culture are collected privately.

In the old Soviet Union, by contrast, culture was an integral part of the state ideology – or anyway, that was the intention. Even there, the most interesting culture balanced in the borderland between the permitted and the forbidden while receiving state aid. Vysotsky sang a dirge for the official Soviet Union on the stage of Taganka long before Gorbachev came to pow-

◀◀ *Exhibition of Professor Timo Sarpaneva's works in the Finnish Embassy in Washington. Timo Sarpaneva's archives.*

▶ *The* Orchid *vase was declared the world's most beautiful object by* House Beautiful Magazine *in 1954.*

er. We have been able to watch the liberating impact of glasnost for more than ten years.

There are countries in which the national culture is nurtured as a monument of bygone glory, and then there are countries which have discovered a new identity through the national culture after losing great-power status.

And then again, Finland has adopted a system whereby the public authority pays for most of the piping, but the pipers decide for themselves what to play. In other words, there are both state support and freedom of choice, an altogether luxurious arrangement. The reality of life is different especially in the field of cultural exports, where the Ministry for Foreign Affairs is active. There the public message and the wishes of sponsors are combined in a way that suits both sides.

It is my impression that the division of roles between the public and private sectors is only beginning. For example, there are fields in which companies subsidize museums but the public sector supports exports instead of the reverse. It is often the case in the field of cultural exports that the consolidation of private and public cultural inputs to maximize the overall effect is a mere wish.

On the other hand, it is hardly surprising that the result is like a man in a blindfold, since the public sector first arranges the financing and then sets about making the product, whereas the private sector will only finance a ready-made product. It may be that the encounter also has innovative features. But there is the danger that, unless a real encounter takes place, one side will start to think for the other. People in the public sector wonder if the business community is unable to understand what is for its own best, while companies think they have already done their part once by paying tax money. Besides which, many Finnish companies are in doubt as to the wisdom of declaring themselves nationally partial at all in this age of globalization.

On the other hand, I believe I have found signs of increasingly open national declaration in recent years, perhaps partly because of the way Finland came through the severe economic trials of the early 1990s in the forefront of those countries meeting the euro criteria has stirred widespread admiration, and public authority has played a part in this, which is in itself also a cultural act. It is good to be able to identify oneself with success; it is a source of synergy.

Some years ago, my wife and I acted as the honorary hosts at a fund-raising event for the US National Symphony Orchestra. This was practically the city's only white-tie ball of the year, so it was a highly dignified occasion of its kind. The sum collected for the orchestra came to two and a half million marks, mainly from the business community. While I was preparing to report to President Bush and his wife, who had been patrons for the occasion, on the relationship between public authority and culture in Finland, I asked the Finnish Ministry of Education how much money was used for this. The ministry did its best, but the correct figure could not be discovered.

When official artists' posts had been added in but the regular support for the educational institution was deducted, we finally came to a figure that was in excess of one per cent of Finland's gross domestic product. The equivalent sum for the USA would be roughly seventy billion dollars. Among the Americans who believed in and worked hard for private financing, this figure attracted great delight and even admiration for Finland's responsible policy on culture. I wonder what the figure today might be, now that the GDP has expanded, the budget frozen, the number of cultural institutions has grown and sponsorship has come into the picture.

After working for some time in the USA, where market forces predominate, I became convinced that culture undoubtedly acts as a force multiplier on the capability of a small country.

But what is the feature that needs to be focused on in a national culture so that synergy can be found? In my opinion it is quality and the insight referred to by Revel. Here are a few examples from real life.

At the beginning of the decade, we arranged a Helen Schjerfbeck exhibition in Washington, and a third of her works at the Ateneum gallery were shipped over. We arranged space for this national treasure of ours at the only appropriate museum, the Phillips Gallery, whose own collection centred on French *fin de siècle* art. It was a handsome exhibition, but the otherwise copious critiques were hesitant. To my astonishment, it became clear that the critiques had no terms of reference: no Schjerfbeck works had been acquired by the major collections in America. We were exhibiting our national heritage, but Americans came to see an unknown Finnish artist's work whose output and life story struck a chord. The message got through: 50,000 people came to the exhibition.

I will now refer to an example of quality, also from real life. In the early 1990s a new Finnish embassy was built in Washington DC. This included an office with a certain number of square metres per employee. I hoped that the building would become the face of modern Finland in the New World. The architects, however – Markku Komonen and Mikko Heikkinen – did not have Finnishness in mind; they created a good and beautiful building. Quality became the common thread. The investment turned out to be well worthwhile. "At last, something fresh in Washington architecture," enthused the Washington Post. "The best building in Washington in 50 years", began an article in an architects' journal. The grand old man of architecture I.M. Pei asked to look at the building as "I have myself built a building or two in Washington in the past half-decade." The final seal of approval came in the first page of the introduction to *The Architecture of Diplomacy* by Jane Loeffler, published this spring, "Everyone sees the building as a diplomatic bull's-eye for Finland. Looking around the building, one notices immediately that Finland is a totally modern place, everything in the building is high tech, and the quality of the work and Finnish design stand out above all else. A single glance gives a better impression of Finland than dozens of pamphlets, books, films, tourist advertisements and official exchange programmes." Even Finnish openness, one of the key objectives of our EU policy at the Amsterdam summit, received special mention.

Before we fall over to congratulate ourselves, let us remember that the Finnishness of the building was an afterthought. This is what happens when basic, national values are respected. There was no need to stress the point; the Finnishness is in the eye of the beholder. Public authority created national culture, with insight and without additional expense.

My third example is related to the concept of a meeting place I referred to earlier. When our building was declared a national landmark it immediately became a meeting place. When the construction work was completed, a national cultural project began. The first major effort was a retrospective exhibition of Timo Sarpaneva, which was attended by 10,000 people in a month and a half. The multiplier effect of the building works superbly, tickling people's curiosity in advance. Once again, national culture was the result.

Finally, I will close with a short anecdote. It turned out that the godmother of the wife of my American opposite number, Deputy Secretary of State Talbott, was the American design guru Elizabeth Gordon, who in the early 1950s made Sarpaneva famous in the USA by declaring his *Orchid* vase the world's most beautiful object of 1954 in her *House Beautiful* magazine. A glimpse of the tearful reunion of Gordon and Sarpaneva was shown on the evening news in the USA, but hopefully the full twenty minutes of it is in the Finnish Broadcasting Company's archives as part of the story of Finnish design and the substance of national culture.

"National culture and internationational capital".
Seminar 10 November 1998.
Sectretary of State Jukka Valtasaari

Osmo Thiel

The Future of Design

In *The Future of Aesthetics* (1998), Francis Sparshott, a Canadian philosopher and researcher in aesthetics, claims that this future is dependent on the future of philosophy, in turn contingent upon the development of the universities. For Sparshott, the main issue is the role of the research university in creating "a map of knowledge". By a map, he means the classification of material pertaining to a specific area – in aesthetics the systematic classification of the arts. The future of aesthetics is thus entailed in the future of philosophy and by extension in the future of society itself, in which the universities and research play an important role.

In a similar vein, it can be suggested that the applied arts, such as architecture and design, depend on the overall development of the fine arts and culture, as also on the universities and their research efforts. The role of higher institutes of learning in the arts is different. They do not produce maps of knowledge, but will lend support to the expression and skills of the individual. They will produce "maps of skills", whereby the individual can chart the relationships of knowledge and skills by analysing and viewing the world primarily through action and the realm of skills.

Aesthetics has traditionally studied the domain of philosophy associated with the arts and the concept of beauty. Surprisingly, design and the study of aesthetics have had very little to do with each other. Design research has largely borrowed its approaches from history, sociology and semiotics, and more recently from economics.

All in all, there has been relatively little research concerning design – this map of knowledge mostly remains to be constructed. In the Finnish context, even the so-called golden age of design of the 1950s and '60s, and its underlying reasons, are largely uncharted. The map of skills of that period is known to many, but an extensive analysis, a scholarly mapping, is for the most part unavailable. Such knowledge, however, would help a great deal in outlining the future and in understanding the course of developments.

Without doubt, the main factor contributing to the international success of the golden age of Finnish design was the uncompromising effort of gifted designers combined with the significant role of H. O. Gummerus, managing director of the Finnish Society of Crafts and Design as a cultural envoy and protagonist of design. But what was the role of education – the then Institute of Arts and Crafts? What was the function of support from the state and demand from society after the second world war? How did functionalism and modernism promote the emergence of "Finnish" design? Was Marimekko more of a popular movement and a social and cultural actor than a business involved in marketing and design?

Many of these questions are still open. Perhaps because, paraphrasing Sparshott, the chains of interaction are so extensive that a focus on applied arts or design alone would be insufficient. What is needed is an interdisciplinary perspective together with an understanding of relationships of cause and effect.

The purpose of mapping is always to chart the unknown, the *terra incognita*. This book, too, seeks to find and combine the national and international features, phenomena and persons who have figured in the emergence and evolution of the concept known as Finnish design.

▶ *Stefan Lindfors (born 1962), The* Abacus *chair, 1999, P. O. Korhonen.*

Anna-Leena Hakatie (born 1965), Kupla *tumblers and a pourer, 1997, Iittala.*

Iittala

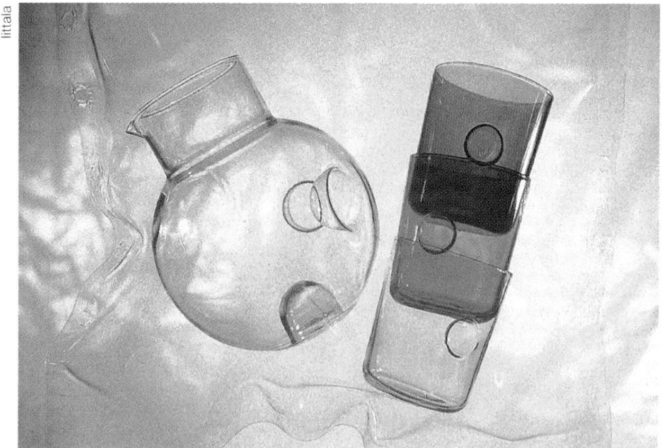

Blowing device Proflow 3, *1998. Muodos Oy, Kemira Safety Oy.*

Muodos/Sami Kulju

Snowcrash/Valvomo

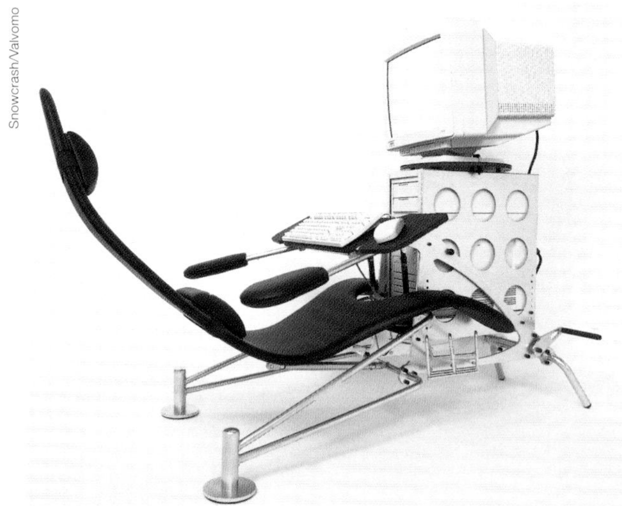

Netsurfer *1996, the Snowcrash group.*

T. Salli

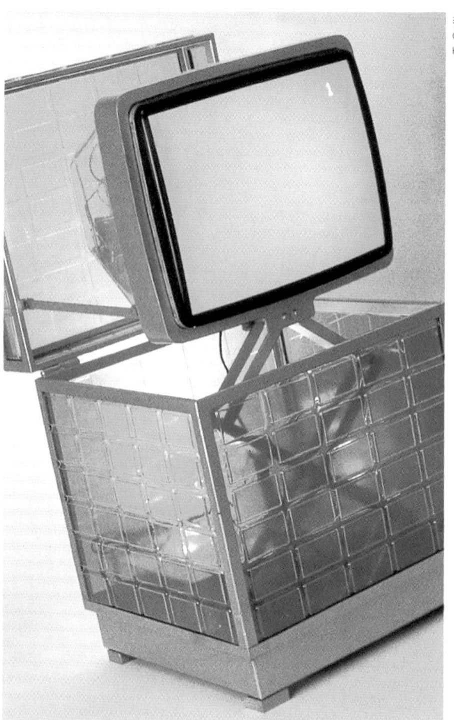

Timo Salli (born 1963), Jack-in-the-box, *1996, prototype.*

Although Sparshott's conception of the research university as the prime mover of the future is by no means novel, it is correct, for the universities have a key role in future developments. They will create opportunities, or will fail to do so. The most important resources of network society and globalized competition are information and its availability. In the future, education and research will constitute important national and private capital.

In seeking to outline the future of design we need information on the past, on successes and failures. We need history and its analyses, the map of knowledge of the past. But this alone is not enough for assessing the future. We also need a perceptive analysis of the present and its phenomena – and above all we need the young designers who will shape the future. Also for these reasons, institutes of higher learning play an important role in offering points of departure for the makers and creators of the future.

▶ *Pasi Pänkäläinen (born 1964),* Chair 022, *1997, Piiroinen.*

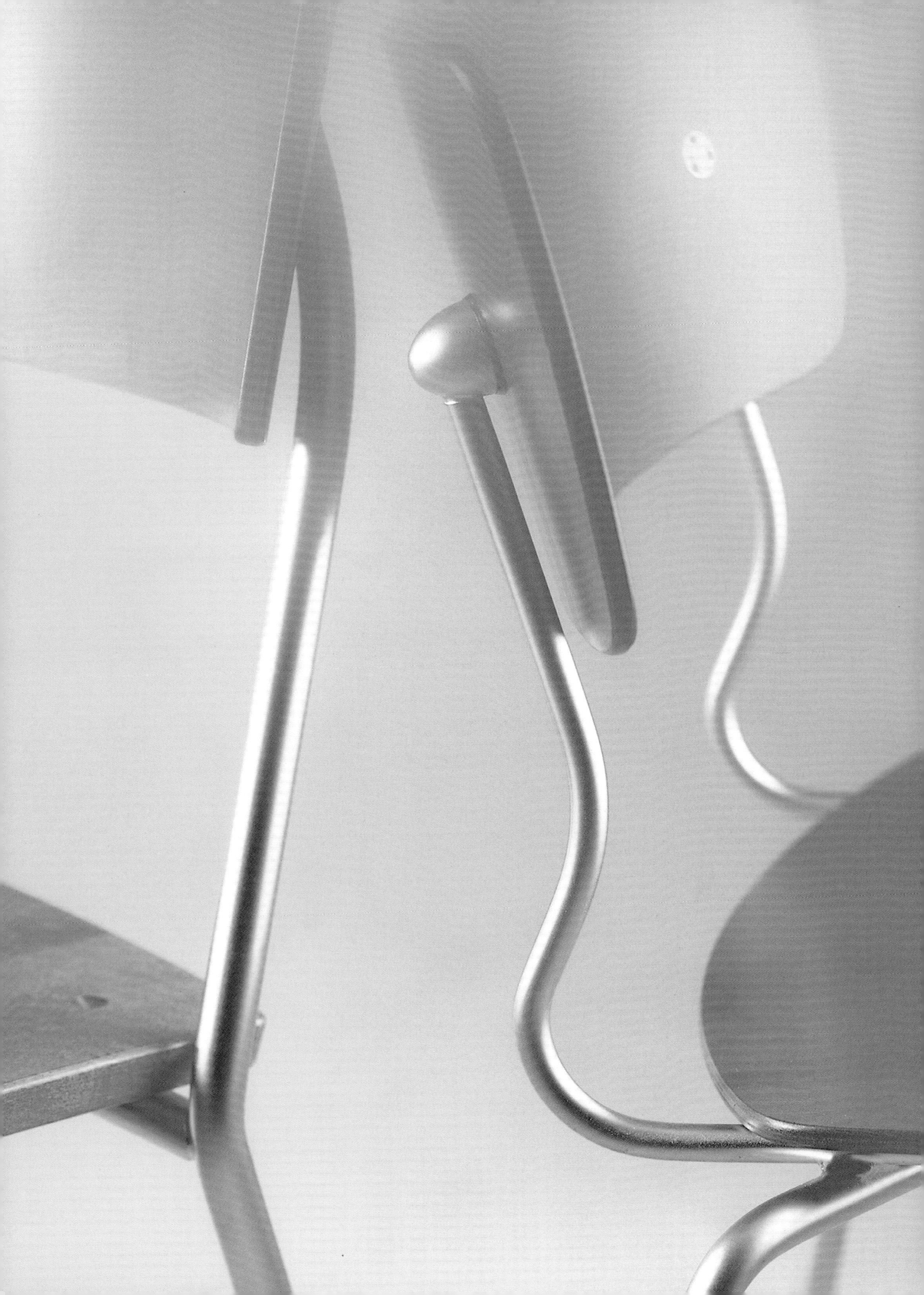

Piiroinen

Sari Anttonen (born 1966), the Kiss *chair, 1998, Piiroinen.*

Harri Koskinen (born 1970), Candle lantern, 1999, Relations/Iittala.

Iittala

Cappellini

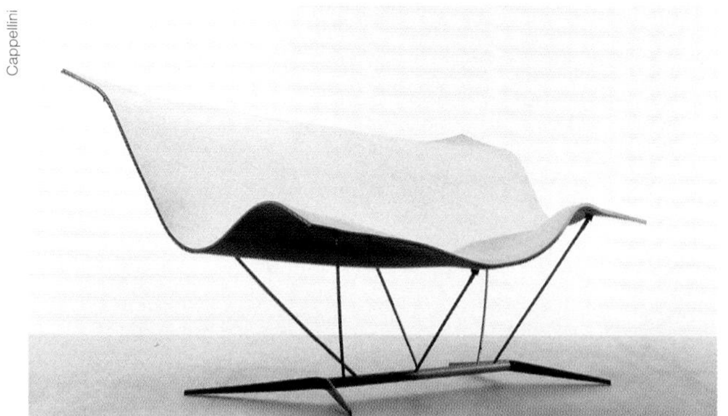

Ilkka Suppanen (born 1968), Flying Carpet *Sofa, 1998, Cappelini.*

Snowcrash/Valvomo

Glowblow *lamp, 1996, Snowcrash-group.*

The future of design is depends on upon a continuous re-evaluation of the past, on future designers and the overall development of culture and society.

Designers and artists do not work alone. They need orders, commissions, critics and those who understand them. The functioning of all the background factors is a necessary condition for success on the part of an individual designer. The future of design requires co-operation across the board, involving design education, design organizations, designers, researchers, critics, the press, the business community and the public. Also in the background are the state and society. It is through the functioning of this complex network that Finnish design – and its future – are created.

Helsinki, 20 July 1999
Anne Stenros

▶ *Stefan Lindfors (born 1962),* EgO *cup 1998, Arabia. This cup was designed in honour of the 125th anniversary of the Arabia factory.*

The National Context

Ritva Wäre

The national character of visible form is often associated with the national aspect of production, the domestic nature of architecture and utility objects, and varied objectives relating to exports. Political situations and goals also shape the development of designed form. identifiable national design is often assumed to reveal the solid cultural background, long history or spiritual strength of a people. The characteristics of national identity can be discussed and debated, but it defies definition. At the turn of the 19th and 20th centuries there were even attempts to find scholarly proof of Finnishness in form and style, but these efforts were widely debated and they never came to completion. However, over the years certain features and the works of certain designers came to be regarded as more Finnish than others. In this context, Finnishness was defined within a process of social contracts greatly influenced by contemporary and later interpretations.

Finnish architecture and applied arts of the turn of the last century are customarily, though not quite accurately, termed national-romantic, because the concept of a national character of design was particularly prominent at the time. In reality, however, discussion on the national character of design left only few marks on artistic design as such and even these few traces were mixed with a variety of international influences. Fin-de-siècle discussion on Finnishness, experiments in design and the new architecture and applied arts have nevertheless shaped the conceptions of later periods about the specifically Finnish nature of design.

As is well known, a distinctly Finnish culture was developed and strengthened throughout the 19th century, while Finland, an autonomous Grand Duchy of the Russian Empire, became increasingly independent in economic and intellectual terms, gradually maturing to political independence, which was achieved in 1917. The process of achieving independence in architecture and applied arts were strongest in the 1890s and at the turn of the century. Other areas of the arts, literature, music and the visual arts – and their great masters – achieved national independence earlier.

Throughout the 19th century it was repeatedly underlined that Finland still had much to achieve in all areas of intellectual life in comparison with the so-called great cultural nations. This particularly concerned architecture and applied arts. The overall objective of cultural policies was to make Finland progress apace with the western nations. Even in the early 1890s it was suspected that Finns did not have any sense of form or abilities in the visual arts. In his introduction to the first general work on Finnish art, the art historian Eliel Aspelin wrote that conditions in Finland were not conducive to the visual arts: "Here, where the gloom and darkness of winter predominates through most of the year, and even during the brief summer the air is rarely clear and truly translucent, the eye will not become accustomed to viewing the forms of objects in the same way as in the south." Aspelin noted the point, often repeated by others, that Finns were more prone to study the internal rather than the superficial aspects of phenomena, which made poetry closer to them than arts in which "form and the accuracy and grace of contour were the main consideration". Limited natural resources, e.g. the lack of sandstone and marble, the former lack of political independence and poverty had prevented the visual arts from becoming established and from developing independently.

▶ *Herman Gesellius, Armas Lindgren and Eliel Saarinen, 1901–1903, office and residential buildings of Hvitträsk, Kirkkonummi.*

Rauno Träskelin

During the years that followed, in the 1890s and at the turn of the century, the concepts of new, original and Finnish became ambiguously intertwined in architecture and applied arts. The rapid pace of developments is reflected by the fact that in the early 1900s Finns would celebrate their architects and designers whose works were presented abroad, in Scandinavian journals and, for example, in German publications such as *Dekorative Kunst* and *Moderne Bauformen*. The new Finnish architecture had become a concept in its own right by this stage. It was Finland's contribution to the achievements of European art of the close of the century and it was felt to have sprung from a national spirit, as noted by the Finnish architect Jac. Ahrenberg in 1904. While architecture became an important element of the external image of the nation, it also began to interest the domestic public.

The "Finnish architecture" of the early 1900s did not evolve in isolation or "come about as if by magic", even though contemporary comments would often lapse into such exaggeration. Generally speaking, it can be described as a Finnish variant of international art nouveau, which was developed at all stages with international trends and concepts in mind. The very con-

◀ *Hvitträsk the "tupa" living room of Eliel Saarinen's residence.*

▶ *Herman Gesellius, Armas Lindgren and Eliel Saarinen, the* Koti *(Home) couch which won a prize in the furniture competition arranged by the Friends of Finnish Handicraft, 1897.*

cept of a nationality for form or style was an internationally shared idea, on the basis of which various national styles had been developed in many European countries. The most influential of these was the so-called German Renaissance style. Finnish architects were also familiar with the Russian style and the Ancient Nordic styles of Sweden and Norway, which found expression particularly in timber architecture and applied arts. In this respect, Finland can be regarded as a kind of intermediary zone, where the achievements and developments of its neighbours in architecture and applied arts were well known. Early Finnish experiments in a specific national style were carried out in 1885 when the Tsar and Tsarina visited the country and in 1889 in the interior design of the Imperial fishing cottage at the Langinkoski rapids near Kotka. These achievements can be regarded as Finnish versions of the widespread Russian national style. The experiments in timber architecture and interior design of the 1890s which sought to develop a specifically Finnish style had many external features in common with similar architecture and design in Norway, Sweden and Russia. These included general rustic characteristics, bare log walls, unpainted furniture and various types of carved ornament. Vernacular embroidery patterns in bright colours on a light surface predominated in textiles. Although differences arose from the national background of forms and ornamental motifs, it can be claimed that ultimately the same North European style was present.

Germany was an important mediator of new European concepts and ideas. It was also a major source of impulses, whose industrial production led to reactions in many neighbouring countries and served to promote trends towards national production and style. The applied arts objects imported into Finland and the architecture of German design books were regarded as examples of fatigue in design, lethargy and degenerated taste. The opposite was found in the trend influenced by the English arts and crafts movement, regarded as new and sound. Commenting in 1898 on Christmas window displays in the centre of Helsinki, Jac. Ahrenberg noted how all the poor specimens of applied arts and trash that could not be exported to America or the exotic lands of Africa were now marketed in Finland. He complained that the Finns sought to learn from the Germans in all areas. In the same year Acke Andersson wrote an article on tiled stoves for the new *Ateneum* magazine, in which he commented that the German Renaissance should be steered back to Germany "the fatherland of sausage and beer

Herman Gesellius, Armas Lindgren and Eliel Saarinen, the Finland Pavilion in the Paris world's fair in 1900. The frescoes of the entrance hall were painted by Axel Gallén.

Museum of Finnish Architecture

steins". Opinions and comments on German architecture and industry were common in Finland throughout the years around the turn of the century. It was to replace the "galloping Germanic spirit", that something new and Finnish was needed, as noted by the sculptor Emil Wikström when he urged Axel Gallén to participate in a design competition held by the Friends of Finnish Handicraft.

Where the German influence was regarded as representing the trash and trinket industry and period styles in architecture, everything that came from England was raised on a pedestal. English architecture and applied arts had a considerable influence in almost all countries in Europe, and they were studied intensively enough in Finland at the turn of the century. For example, in 1909 Dr. Yrjö Hirn held a public lecture on William Morris's theory of "artistic crafts". The lecture was arranged by the Finnish Society of Crafts and Design. The English influence included an interest in medieval arts and crafts, an appreciation of individual craftsman-

Museum of Finnish Architecture

ship and the revival of old materials and techniques. Architecture stressed the relationship of buildings with their surroundings and the use of local building materials. The English influence was most prominent in the area of so-called "home art", which included houses and interior design. A new feature was a focus on the art of the everyday sphere and the daily milieu of people, with the overall goal of making life a thing of beauty and simplicity. As noted by the artist Albert Edelfelt in 1898, the underlying concept of the new movement, the "art nouveau", was to make beauty available to everyone and to extend the sphere of art down to the smallest details of the environment. This concept entailed an expansion of the traditional professional domains of artists and architects. Visual artists would design houses and their interiors and would be active in various sectors of applied arts. The work of architects would extend to interior design and objects of art and crafts on the one hand, and extensive town-planning projects on the other.

The term art nouveau, the new art, first appeared in Finnish publications in 1898 in reference to a broad European reform movement in art and architecture. It encompassed the principles of English design, Henry van de Velde's work in Belgium, the Austrian secession, and art nouveau in the limited sense of the word, implying Horta's and Hankar's designs in Belgium and contemporary developments in France. This reform movement was generally met in a positive vein. Art nouveau overshadowed the former debate on the correct points of departure for a national style. It also made it clear that architects or artists in general did not have to conform to any style. Writing in 1901, the architect Bertel Jung observed: "The style worship of recent times is now countered with the rule that no styles are to be followed and that everyone must create things on their own, keeping to general and economic principles."

In all its variety, Finnish art nouveau evolved within a distinct international framework, and it can be regarded as one of the manifestations of international art nouveau. It was marked by a tendency towards Finnish originality. This influence naturally varied even during a brief period, above all according to the personality of designers. In the following section I analyse these elements of design that can be described as Finnish, and the concepts and patterns of thought underlying their use.

Finnish wood

The idea of developing an explicitly Finnish style of timber architecture was broached in the early 1890s. This was partly associated with older convergent tendencies in applied arts and interior design, and especially with the design competitions organized by the Friends of Finnish Handicraft. It was also noted that competitions should be held for the design of buildings in the Finnish style: "Such [competitions] would bring forth all that the spirit of our nation has created and thus we will perhaps see the day when houses are built – both on the outside and the inside – also in the Finnish style." (Architect Vilho Penttilä 1894). Here, the objective of Finnishness was generally associated with the reform of wooden architecture. Something genuine and honest was desired to replace the weatherboarded and richly decorated wooden buildings of the so-called "carpenter style". There was a need for something in which the wooden material and the structure employed would be clearly present and the decoration would have some organic connection with the building as a whole. It had to conform to the nature of timber and not imitate the shapes and forms of architecture in stone. Around this time, a number of Finnish carpentry factories sought to develop exportable wooden houses in accordance with foreign examples, which may have spurred the need to develop unique and original architecture in wood.

According to the prevailing view, the most original forms, and ornaments in particular, had survived in popular art. The problem with Finland, however, was that there was hardly any vernacular tradition of wooden architecture that could have been revived or whose features could directly be taken as examples. The vernacular architecture of Finland was modest and unassuming in its forms. Predominating in the countryside were simple corner-joined log houses with saddle-back roofs, and interesting ornamental forms were only to be found in the carved consoles of outbuildings and storehouses. This aspect of folk culture had not yet been studied in detail, but the most fervent Finnish-

A chair designed by Axel Gallén at the Iris factory stand of the Paris World Fair.

minded elements felt that the folk culture of Western Finland was dominated by Swedish influences, and could thus not be the basis of a Finnish style. These attitudes were soon toned down, and by the first decade of the 20th century, the folk art of Southern Ostrobothnia, in the west, was eagerly studied. At this stage, and partly previously, vernacular *ryijy* (*rya*) rugs from various parts of the country began to interest designers.

The early stages of developing a Finnish style led only to a few experiments. However, it brought to the tore log-built and unboarded vernacular buildings in general, and various types of storehouses in particular. Since then, the unfaced and unpainted log wall and the themes and motifs of the two-storey loft storehouses have belonged to the repertoire of Finnish architecture that is regarded as specifically Finnish. Villas were built with a hall or living room resembling the all-purpose room, or *tupa*, of the farmhouses. These rooms in the villas also had bare log walls, visible ceiling and roof structures and an open fireplace. Additional support for this type of room was found in English dwellings. Generally speaking, developments at the turn of the 19th and 20th centuries presented to the public unfaced and unpainted timber in its assumedly original simplicity.

Karelian motifs

Applications of East Karelian timber architecture and ornamental motifs and discussion concerning their significance and meaning were closely associated with the above work of developing the timber style. This phenomenon was part of the romantic Karelia-oriented enthusiasm, or Karelianism, of the intelligentsia and artists. Although it had little practical impact on architecture, Karelianism was a prominent movement, owing to which later writings cited Karelia as an important influence on architecture and applied arts. The fashion of the turn of the century of using unfaced and round logs was partly due to the influence of East Karelian architecture. The round logs gave the exterior a feeling of strength and weight, while projecting an archaic impression. Architects also applied the impressive gable structures of the Karelian houses and their projecting eaves, which helped give the wooden buildings an air of grandeur.

Round logs, steep roofs with wide eaves and windows with small panes were expressive themes in log villas designed by Lars Sonck. Also at Hvitträsk, the studio and residence designed by the architects Herman Gesellius, Armas Lindgren and Eliel Saarinen for their own use, these features were important motifs until the walls were faced with shingles at a later stage. With the exception of round logs, the studio-villas designed by the artists Emil Wikström, Axel Gallén (later Gallen-Kallela) and Pekka Halonen for their own use had many features freely referring to the Karelian houses.

Finnish ornament

Already in the 1880s Finnish and Karelian vernacular textile ornaments provided a basis for textile design to give products a specifically Finnish flavour. The Friends of Finnish Handicraft association, founded in 1879, was responsible for these activities, ranging from textiles to the design of ancient-style jewellery and home interiors in the "Finnish style". The mostly geometric Karelian textile ornaments were of interest because scholars also assumed them to contain the most authentic and original features of Finnish folk art. In Western Finland, however, ornament also reflected western influence more than "national authenticity". The straight lines and simplicity of geometric ornaments was assumed to express the Finnish temperament.

Geometric ornament was applied extensively in the 1890s in carpentry and cabinet making, furniture, textiles, jewellery, ceramics, decorative painting and graphics. There were also occasional discussions on the suitability of Finnish ornament in polychrome brick architecture. Vilho Penttilä wrote an article on this subject after seeing contemporary brick architecture at the Berlin Industry Fair of 1896. This idea, however, could not even be technically realized, because façade brick acceptable for the purpose could not yet be made in

Finland. There was also architectural debate on whether ornamental motifs alone made a building or style Finnish, if such a goal was even necessary. The journalist Kasimir Leino noted bluntly that Finnish ornamental motifs could not be adopted directly from "towels" to contemporary applied arts. Moreover, at the very turn of the century, comparative studies showed how widespread and universal these assumedly Finnish geometric motifs in fact were.

The Middle Ages

The medieval heritage had fascinated European authors, artists and architects throughout the 19th century. In discussions on the genuinely Finnish aspects of the architectural heritage, medieval churches and castles were observed to be problematic, for they represented Swedish rule and foreign cultural influence in general. This uncompromising attitude was matched by broader views according to which tradition had sanctified the Finnish nature of the medieval churches over time. In broader perspective, the Nordic nature of these buildings was admired and they were regarded as the independent local versions of the major churches of Central Europe, created by the artist-builders of the Middle Ages. Medieval churches were studied and documented, for example by artists, and their motifs and themes were occasionally repeated in contemporary church architecture. Individual motifs from castles were used emblematically in new housing architecture, whose predominant features, however, derived from the English context.

Medieval buildings and crafts influenced the fashion of vaulted interiors with painted groins, solid, low cylindrical columns, windows with round and tapering arches and large open fireplaces. Stained glass techniques and wrought-iron work were also revived. Solid, heavy forms and unpainted wood were popular in furniture design. The examples for design were not sought in the historical architecture or the few surviving medieval objects of the Finnish context. In the background was the whole realm of international medieval and medievalist material providing the parameters within which design could proceed freely, seeking a general medieval tone.

Admiration for the medieval period and a search for its mood and ambience partly influenced the widespread use of domestic natural stone around the turn of the century. This, too, involved a fashion that had spread throughout Europe, favouring the use of unhewn stone in façades. The examples for this were adopted from abroad, primarily from the neo-romanesque natural stone architecture developed by H. H. Richardson in the United States. Although the examples and prototypes of design came from abroad, the

Department of Museums/P. O. Welin

The interior of Lohja Church. The church was built in the Middle Ages.

Central Archives of Fine Arts/Pirje Mykkänen

Axel Gallén, the Defence of the Sampo. *A sketch for the frescos of the Paris World Fair pavillion, 1900. Antell collection, the Art Museum of the Ateneum.*

use of Finnish stone was valuable from the national point of view. The state and Finland's developing stone-working industry sought in all ways to promote the use of domestic stone in both buildings and interiors, and it was in this process that Finnish granite and steatite became sanctified national features, a status which they still appear to enjoy.

Nature as the starting point

Around the turn of the 19th and 20th centuries, various nature-based motifs and themes were perhaps the most popular ones in buildings and in crafts and applied arts objects. Their adoption was associated with the introduction of art nouveau in its Central European form. The domestic background of natural motifs imbued a sufficient degree of Finnishness to works, making it possible to regard a building or textile design as both Finnish and an example of the most recent international trends. The ambiguousness of forms was suited to most building projects, for which a distinct political brand was not desired. For example, geometric ornaments adopted earlier in the 1890s were associated with the pro-Finnish *Fennoman* movement, which in turn prevented their wider use.

Two projects, the Finland Pavilion at the Paris World Fair of 1900 and the Pohjola Insurance Company building in Helsinki, made natural themes and motifs known to the general public. Both were designed by the architects Herman Gesellius, Armas Lindgren and Eliel Saarinen. The main features of the Finland Pavilion were laid down in an architectural competition held for the project in 1898. As previously, a world fair was a very important venue for projecting the image of Finland. The Paris World Fair of 1900 was a kind of review of the civilized world as it existed at the time. Non-participation would have signalled a rejection of one's place among the "family of nations", as was noted in the Finnish press in early 1898. It was obviously important for the future development of design that the separate pavilion of the Grand Duchy of Finland was to be as modern as possible in its design, so that it could be regarded as an example of art nouveau from the outset. International exhibition architecture of the late 19th century followed two courses: one that presented progress and made prominent use of new materials and structural solutions, and another line that presented the specific national character of a country, often employing means associated with history. Accordingly, exhibition pavilions could be based on the national architectural heritage, or they could be outright replicas of important buildings.

The low overall shape of the Finland Pavilion, its steep roof, tower and walls imitating natural stone were faintly reminiscent of rural churches in Finland. The building had two portals of natural stone, which had already been included in the competition brief as examples of the Finnish stone-working industry. Already at an early stage, these round-arched portals were recognized as "American", with reference to American architecture in natural stone. The main theme of the interior was the central hall under the tower, with ceiling frescoes by Axel Gallén on themes from the Kalevala. The frescoes were framed by painted groins of medieval appearance, giving the building an ecclesiastical medieval tone. The woodwork of the doors and showcases with their curving shapes represented art nouveau in its Belgian form. Most of the ornamental motifs were based on natural forms from the flora and fauna of Finland. Pine cones and branches were used in various parts of the building. On the rood, at the foot of the tower, were four sculptures of bears. The stone portals were decorated with chains of bear-heads, squirrels and conifer branches. On the bas-relief tiles between the windows were frogs on lily-pads. On the exterior were lynx and elk's head motifs and eagle designs. While domestic, these natural themes were also in use in many other countries. For example the pine branch and the cone were common features in both German and Swedish design.

Contemporary writers recognized the varied meanings of the pavilion and its genius of compromise. It was a creation that had "sprung from the soil of Finland", while it was also art nouveau and an example of individual design, as noted by the architect Gustaf Strengell in 1903. The architect and art critic Sigurd Frosterus commented in 1905 that the concept of a national style was a kind of overcoat under which originally foreign concepts were presented.

With support from the example set by the pavilion domestic nature motifs came into widespread use in architecture, interior design and applied arts products. The steatite façades of the Pohjola Insurance Company building, completed in 1901, and the ornamentation of its interior included not only mythological motifs but also so many themes from the flora and fauna of Finland that contemporaries discussed whether its style should be called Finnish-Naturalist. One critic said that the house brought to mind a museum of natural history rather than a business edifice.

The most common themes from nature in buildings and applied arts objects were the bear, the fox, the squirrel, the swan, the frog and various hawks and owls. The most popular items of flora were conifers, including juniper, rowan leaves and berries, thistles, dandelions, water-lilies and adder's fern. There were also various algae and lichens, which appeared in often highly stylized form in textiles of the early 20th century. They were free-form designs whose origin was difficult to recognize and whose clumsy execution was also criticized.

Simple, unassuming design

During the 19th century, authors and poets crystallized the idea that Finland was a poor country, whose humble inhabitants lived a modest life with no undue boastfulness. Finland lacked considerable natural resources and the nation had not acquired a rich cultural heritage. All that had been achieved here had been imported and reflected influences from abroad. As mentioned above, it was even asked whether there were any preconditions in Finland for the visual arts. The Finns had grown melancholy and introverted and had channelled their artistic creativity into poetry and music.

From this basis, the simplicity and modesty of design were already defined as especially Finnish properties by contemporary writers of the turn of the century. For example, some critics noted that the National Theatre in Helsinki (built 1902) could have been of a simpler design. The architectural competition for the National Museum in Helsinki was decided in 1902, and the Finnish nature of the winning entry was based on its unassuming, sparse and even barren forms. According to Jac. Ahrenberg, the design by Gesellius, Lindgren and Saarinen did not express any festive mood, but rather "the murmur of the tall pines and the rush of the deep streams" and it was close in spirit to the heavy and melancholy mood of folk songs. In the completed version of the National Museum building these features were no longer as prominent, for the design was developed and altered to a considerable degree after the competition. To make simplicity a laudable quality was in logical connection with international developments, the everyday art of English homes and an opposition to period architecture and bric-a-brac. Of the different variants of international art nouveau, Finnish architects and designers preferred to follow the practical and straightforward approach of names such as Josef Hoffman and Adolf Loos rather than the florid forms of Southern Europe.

Simple and natural design was sometimes associated with an expressive crudity of forms, which was also identified as something especially Finnish. An explicitly archaic treatment of forms was generally regarded as referring to the distant past and perhaps to the world of the Kalevala epic. It was expressed for example in the heavy forms of metalwork, devoid of any refinement, and in the use of only crudely hewn natural stone. Aleksis Kivi's novel *The Seven Brothers* presented a "forest Finnishness" that was regarded as an example of primitive strength. Jac. Ahrenberg was wont to see a kind of Aleksis Kivi style in Valter Thomé's and Karl Lindahl's design of the Technology Students House

Department of Museums

The soapstone portal of the Pohjola insurance company building. Gesellius, Lindgren and Saarinen, 1899–1901.

Department of Museums

Valter Thomé and Kurt Lindahl, Technology Students' House, 1901–1903.

in Helsinki. The exterior of this building was dominated by a heavy granite facing that had been added in the final stages of the design and the interior included, among other features, coarsely shaped granite plinths for the columns. Ahrenberg noted that the architectural design expressed associations with Finnish nature, history and the coarse and unaffected character of the Finnish people. The "national element of architecture" consisted in an exaggeratedly simple and sometimes even rough treatment of form and a bold and markedly personal style.

"It is always said that Finns find inspiration in ice, water and trees. I love nature passionately, but I can't really recall where I caught that drop of creativity. I don't lean against a pine and get ideas from it. I certainly love pines, having done logging work as a young man. I then went off to Karelia to paint watercolours, like Akseli Gallen-Kallela and Louis Sparre did. I had the same basic orientation as they did. It can't really be explained. It is shaped by the allure of Finnish nature, the allure of the wilderness, something whole extending from the earth up into the heavens."
Timo Sarpaneva

Design Forum Finland/Rauno Träskelin

Functionalism and the Aaltos

Pekka Suhonen

Alvar Aalto bought his second car in the year of functionalism's breakthrough, 1928, when he and his family had settled in Turku and his first major work, the Southwestern Finland Agricultural Cooperative Building, with its complex functions, was under way. For Aalto, the car (an American Buick) meant first and foremost freedom to travel, and he undertook trips in Finland and Scandinavia. The car was not a particularly urban feature, as many cars had been acquired by people in the countryside, where Prohibition bootleggers and right-wing thugs of the period gave them a specific role in popular imagery. For Aalto, his car was a practical way to visit building sites and to show foreign visitors around Finland and his own buildings.

Aalto dreamed of a car trip to continental Europe with Aino in 1928, when he had received a travel grant from the Kordelin Foundation, but the time could not be spared. Instead they flew to Paris. By then flying was no longer a great rarity, but mostly Finns travelled by ferry, changing to trains once they reached the continent. The machine culture of the Torchbearers, a young literary coterie of the 1920s, had by then a long established romantic tradition of trains, echoes of popular novels like *La Madone des Sleepings* by Maurice Dekobra. True, Mika Waltari aimed for a modern, visual image in his travelogue *Yksinäisen miehen juna* (Lonely Man's Train), 1929: "How can you love express trains, massive locomotives, clattering rails, rocking wagons, mileposts flashing by, sandy embankments compressed into streaks..."

Aino and Alvar Aalto had flown before, on their honeymoon in 1924: this was then a modern choice, as the Finnish national carrier Aero (now Finnair) had been established the previous year. Even before this, in 1921, Alvar Aalto had written a column in Swedish for the satirical magazine *Kerberos* which, although conceived with humorous intent, is evidently the writer's only point of contact with futuristic ideals – the futurist manifesto had been published eight years before. Aalto refers to the revs of the engine as a high artistic value: "In this figure there is almost more art than in all the watercolours and antique furniture in the

▶ *Alvar Aalto,* Paimio *chair 1932-33, Artek Oy.*

Alvar Aalto Archives

Fokker, an early European passanger plane.

Museum of Finnish Architecture

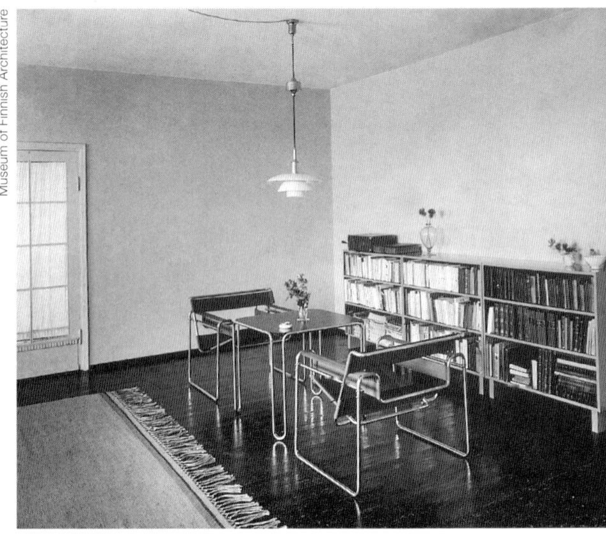

The home of Aino and Alvar Aalto in the Southwestern Finland Agricultural Cooperative Building, late 1920s: Henningsen's PH lamp and Breuer's Wassili chairs.

Alvar Aalto Archives

Aalto's first car was Fiat, 1927.

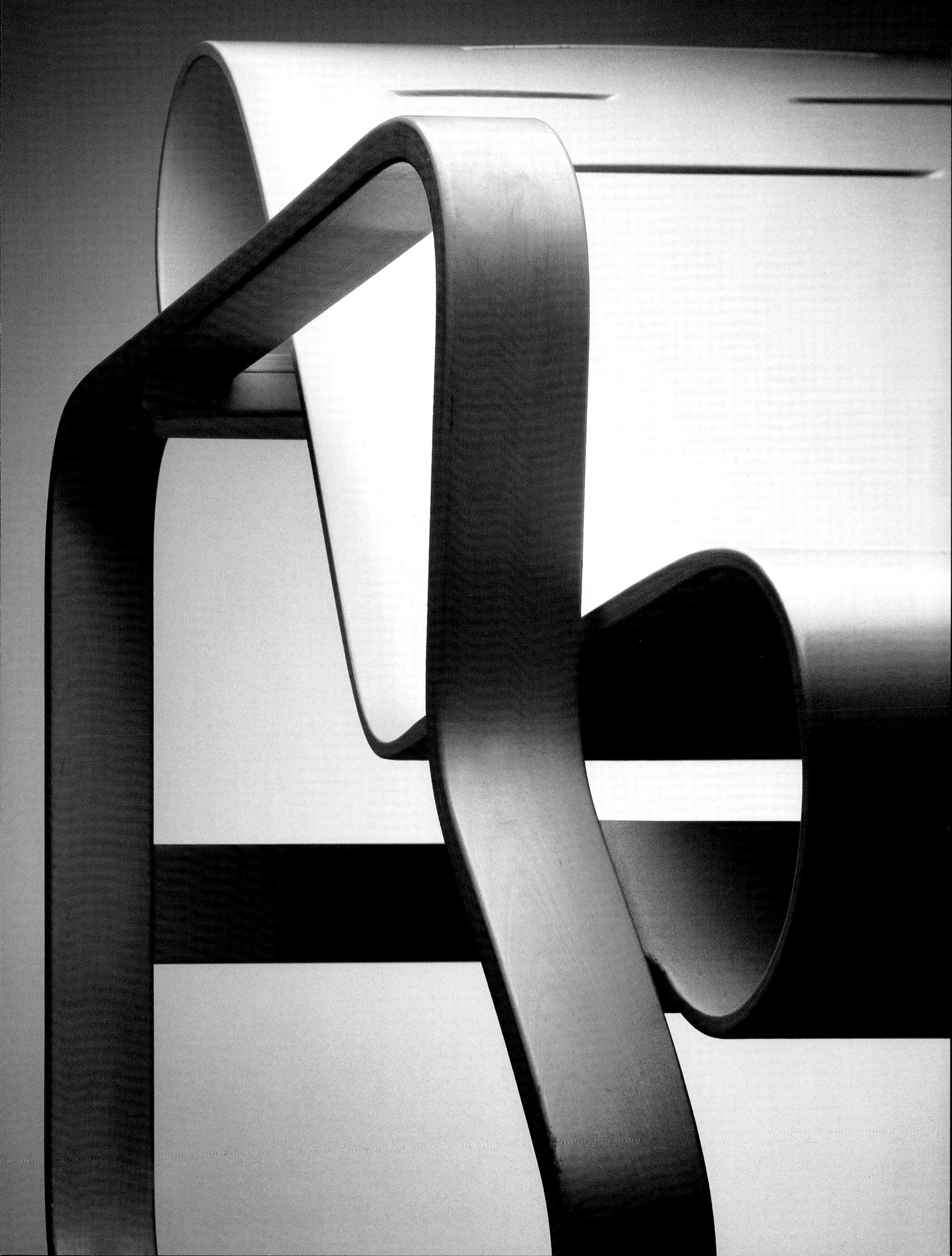

Helsinki City Museum

Jarl Eklund, the Fazer café, Helsinki 1930.

world, to say nothing of porcelain painting." As the pilot of the plane talks with the columnist about town planning in Helsinki, he occasionally has to switch the engine off to hear what is said. Some points of the city are given approval, but "...all the rest of that city built by idiots is going to get blown up when the captain and I are in control." The column was printed before expressionistic modernism emerged in Finland, but machine aesthetics had earlier enthusiasts in Finland, Guss Matsson in his famous columns before the First World War and Sigurd Frosterus during it. In Aalto's later modernistic writings in the late 1920s and early 1930s, there are also references to the practicality, economy, and precision of machines and the appropriacy of their design language. However, he wrote no manifesto for the triumph of technology in the times functionalism was making its breakthrough, let alone later, when he took a critical view of technology's omnipotence and especially of its monomaniac devotees. However, commitment to modernism shows in his interior designs: the Southwestern Finland Agricultural Cooperative Building in Turku, in which the Aaltos lived, had some classicist features, but there were Marcel Breuer steel-tube chairs in the living room, whereas Olavi Paavolainen, who shortly afterwards lived in the Turun Sanomat newspaper office building which was one of Aalto's most orthodox functionalist designs, furnished it with oriental rugs and Turkish smoking-tables. The Torchbearers also steeped their lyricism in both machine romanticism and quasi-oriental exotica at one and the same time.

One of Alvar Aalto's most fertile contacts with 'profound' modernism arose from the encounter with Poul Henningsen of Denmark and his magazine, *Kritisk Revy* (Critical Review). This prepared Aalto for the radical departure of 1927–28. In later years he never commented, or even mentioned in passing, on his classicist buildings of the 1920s, not even in Jyväskylä. He did, however, tell anecdotes about the Jyväskylä of his youth. One gets the undeniable impression that Aalto, having once left behind him a stage that belonged to his youth, never found it necessary to return. Aalto was not alone in this breakthrough, however, as he was a part of a young designers' front. He was flexible and inventive in applying ideas and went on enthusiastically to new things.

Hilding Ekelund, who was subeditor of *Arkkitehti* magazine in 1928, was one of those who belonged to the breakthrough period. He later recalled:

"In Sweden it is customary, when talking of the almost epidemic breakout of functionalism, to say it broke out on the first of February 1928, when the journal Byggmästaren *published its first issue bearing the stamp of the new movement. If we were to express ourselves equally maliciously in Finland, we might say that our functionalism was born on the twenty-first of April the same year, when a distinguished exponent of the tendency, the architect Markelius, expounded the movement's agenda at the annual meeting of the Finnish Association of Architects. The significance of the year 1928 is further emphasized by the fact that the founder of the Bauhaus school, Walter Gropius, visited Stockholm that year to speak on new concepts."*

Although the word functionalism is connected with Le Corbusier, it was used for the first time by Adolf Behne in 1923 in his book Der Moderne Zweckbau (The Modern Practical Building). The same year, Eric Mendelsohn gave a lecture entitled "Dynamik und Funktion". At least at first, Der Funktionalismus was a description of art used in the German-speaking area by those critical of it, one ism among many, and it was initially avoided in architectural circles. But earlier views relating to functionalism are not hard to find even in Finland, although the term itself was not used. During

Helsinki City Museum/A. Pietinen

Werner West, Parliament House café, 1930.

Finland's first modern stage in architecture and applied arts at the turn of the 19th century, they were echoes from continental Europe: the cultural boom in Finland was the result of interaction between continental ideals and Finland's own national aspirations. Finland developed its own, unofficial cultural foreign policy, as was necessary in the political situation at the turn of the century. In the same way, true functionalism in the form it took in Finland in the late 1920s embodied tensions between national and international tendencies, now in politically different circumstances.

The architect Gustaf Strengell, who served in key positions of industrial arts in the early decades of the century, wrote in 1901 of new criteria of beauty, including the concept of C. R. Ashbee's Guild of Handicraft that "the material determines the form". But Strengell did not stop with the ideology of handicrafts, going on to philosophize on mechanical production with the support of Germans and Belgians – chiefly Henri van de Velde. To put it bluntly, he said with van de Velde's mouth: "An artistic product which cannot be reproduced by the hundreds and thousands is worth-

Alvar Aalto archives

The Aaltos' home in Munkkiniemi, Helsinki 1936.

less." Functionalism is expressed in another quote: "A chair is beautiful in so far as it fulfils its function as perfectly as possible. It may be without any kind of decoration, as long as it is comfortable to sit in and it is made in such a way that the functions of its various parts are clearly expressed; as long as it is well 'constructed', it is beautiful."

Strengell's pronouncement precedes in an almost exemplary way the statements with which the modern designers and architects of the 1920s described their aspirations. Another preceding motto from Sweden was 'vackrare vardagsvara' (more beautiful everyday ware), used as the title for a pamphlet on industrial arts by Gregor Paulsson in 1919. This saying was current throughout the functionalist period in the 1930s and was also taken up again later. It was linked with democratic, occasionally – as was the case in Sweden – social democratic priorities in relation to design, architecture, and the people who used these. It was also in touch with another Swedish school of thought in which the language of functionalism was explained in terms of the old, practical principles of folk art and handicrafts and the criteria of beauty which derived – as though automatically – from these. Strengell was attracted by this kind of comparison, at least in 1937 towards the end of his life, when he visited the old Niemelä tenant farm building in the Seurasaari open-air museum in Helsinki, soon after which he went to Alvar Aalto's then fairly new home in Munkkiniemi. He drew parallels between the buildings, their interiors and the atmosphere they evoked.

Alvar Aalto (1896–1976) was not a philosopher, but he was able to pursue philosophical questions in flashes. One such was in 1928 when he attempted to define the new movement in a newspaper interview on New Year's Day: "This 'new realism' –let us call it that now, although the actual phenomenon by its very nature can't be given a proper name – does not add to the number of existing schools of art, having evolved from a systematic attempt to find a reason for the wishy-washy and bloodless art we have today, for changing directions and for rapid obsolescence." Aalto's prediction did not materialize: people in Finland began to use the name functionalism, sometimes calling it rationalism or new objectivism, and a Swedenized slang form, funkis, which was used to mean different things depending on who was talking. Aalto's statement is worth considering in another light, however. The fact that the nature of the new tendency did not require a name – as isms confused the style picture anyway – is, as an idea, close kin to Aalto's pet ideas of 'the little man' or 'the classless society', which also focused on egalitarian anonymity and which appear to have something to do with the perspectives of the Bauhaus school. Actually, Aalto himself – with his characteristic lack of consistency – used the term 'functional architecture' at the end of 1928, but by the idea of keeping the tendency unnamed he seems to have meant its distinct nature in principle from named styles. This is strengthened by the ideas he put forward elsewhere about the profound need to change the entire nature of the architect's work and approach. As Aalto's own aspirations after the breakthrough indicate, the quest for something so absolutely new or also on such a different level that it could not be named in an ordinary context, was linked with his personality, which wanted to astonish rather than submit to something that would congeal into a formula. He did not create the new with words but with actual buildings.

In Sweden, Gotthard Johansson published a book called *Funktionalismen i verkligheten* (Functionalism in Reality) as an after-effect and critique of the Stockholm Exhibition. In the book, he sought to distinguish between 'real' functionalism and the 'funkis' which re-

Alvar Aalto archives

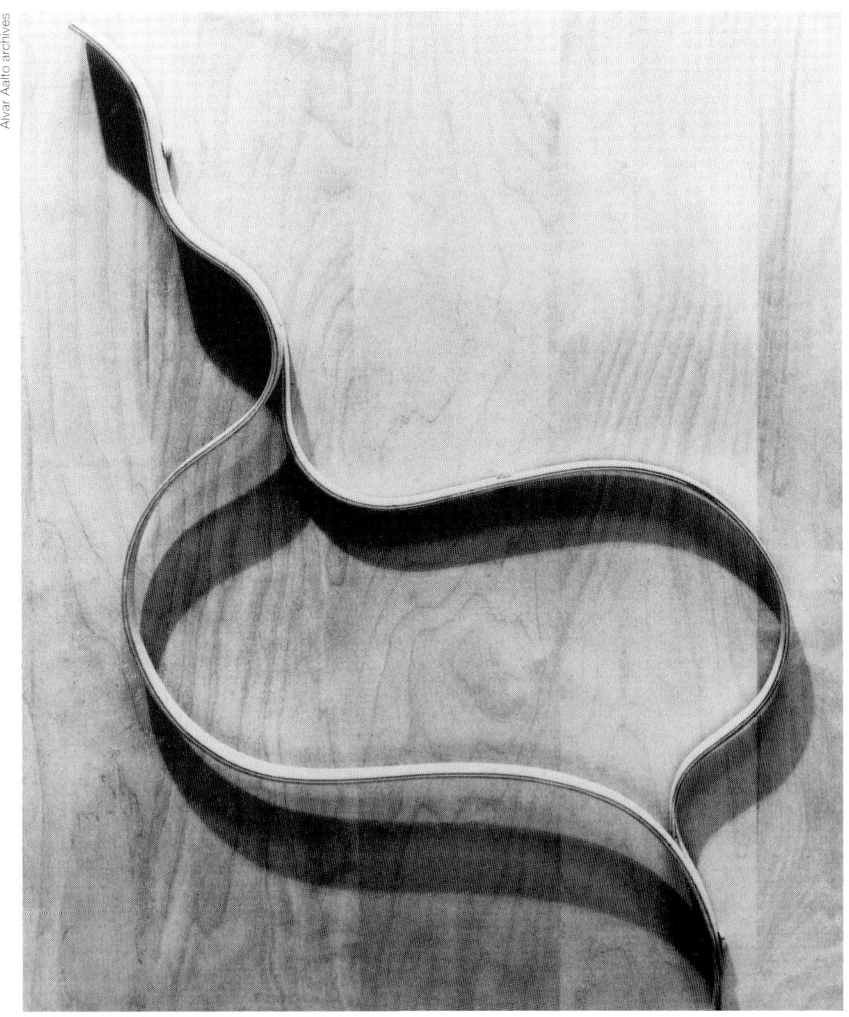

Curved wood design by Alvar Aalto, early 1930s.

sulted in misunderstanding. Real functionalism had started out on a very small scale before the concept had become firmly established. One example from Finland that could be cited is the smallholder's model kitchen by Margaret Nordman (1925), in which she introduced the draining cupboard for dishes that later proved itself a decisive, practical innovation – one which is still mostly unknown in England. Interest in the rational utilization of space had started in Finland before the Stockholm Exhibition of 1930 and a smaller but ideologically important Minimum Apartment Exhibition held in Helsinki the same year. These exhibitions were only a declaration of rationalism, which declaration by 1930 had acquired the name functionalism. The exhibitions had a guiding effect on, for example, Aino Aalto's design work, the independent part of which largely comprised glass objects, furniture, interiors and details: Aino Aalto may be considered a 'true' functionalist who thought about practical needs.

Overall, the new tendency gained ground with apparent ease, especially in architecture, and it had a higher profile in Finland than in several other European countries which had recently become independent, such as Czechoslovakia and Poland, although these countries were interested in functionalism, as they had traditions supported by an existing stock of buildings. The history of design is more open to interpretation. Architectural functionalism, from which design cannot entirely be separated, was not without its opponents in Finland. The most important professorial chair in Finland was awarded in 1931 to J. S. Sirén, who designed the classicist House of Parliament and part of its interior; his only competitor, Aalto, was less experienced, but it also counted against him that the experts were either opposed to functionalism or cautious about it. Among the functionalist camp itself, there was criticism of the fringes: there was a desire to define positions, contents and the image of the tendency within the artistic community. The same could be seen in the industrial arts.

The buildings Chat Doré (1928) designed by Birger Carlstedt and Fazer by Jarl Eklund (1930) were the

Artek

Artek's first shop, Fabianinkatu, Helsinki, 1936.

expressions of modernism most familiar to the general public. These two popular cafés in Helsinki may have been counted as functionalist, although in retrospect they are ambitious Art Deco. Restaurants and barber shops adopted tubular chairs – the fact that they were easy to take care of and hygienic supported this. The shops of the SOK cooperative movement, following the lead of co-ops in Sweden, were given interior design in the modern style in the 1930s. Sirén permitted tubular furniture designed by Werner West (1890–1859) in the Parliament's café, thus making a concession to modernism. However, the ancient dispute between traditional crafts and mass production came to a head in the Finnish Association of Designers Ornamo as late as 1933. Arttu Brummer (1891–1951), a leading figure in industrial design, resigned in mid-term as Ornamo's chairman, writing in the yearbook he edited a vigorous attack on functionalism, mechanization and all manner of 'torchbearing'. By then, the Torchbearers in their original form had already broken up. Brummer advocated individual crafts. His own output was superb in that field, but it was perceived as old-fashioned by the younger set. It involved chairs upholstered with red suede and radio cabinets decorated with ebony and gilding (1928). In the 1930s the Stockmann department store's draughtsman's office, which was run by Werner West, took a favourable view of functionalism, as did the Taito company run by Paavo Tynell. Taito later produced many of Aalto's light fittings. These business enterprises took a moderate line on functionalism. The Merivaara factories also belonged to the functionalist camp because of their tubular furniture, and the 'heteka' steel-tube bed became a must in the homes of young couples. Pauli Blomstedt designed Art Deco-style tubular furniture for Merivaara which departed from preconceived forms and was in some degree formalist: the stylistic idiom was new, however. These objects have gained new popularity in the post-modern period, for example in Italy and the USA.

Alvar Aalto combined the new functionally unchanging demands for interior design and the reinterpretation of the supporting and supported parts of basic functionally unchanging furniture – chairs and tables. His stance is described in a passage published in *Domus* magazine in 1930 under the heading "The Housing Problem". The article deals with the same questions as the Minimum Apartment Exhibition held in Helsinki at the end of the same year. Aalto attempts to explain to the reader what he means by the word culture in connection with housing issues. He too realizes that the concept of culture is not one to be defined by a single sentence and therefore gives an example:

"An ocean liner. The engineer responsible for the working of the ship's turbines is sitting at a desk in his cabin. Along the walls are plotters producing diagrams on the ship's fuel consumption, steam pressure, engine revolutions, various temperatures. The room and the person in it together form a typical organic working unit. It is likely that the person in question is fairly indifferent to the design of his bed and to whether the most fashionable materials have been used for the walls. Instead he attaches great value to the room's informal comfort, his resting posture – and perhaps, as the case may be – to reading a good book. He probably also feels quite warmly about the organic entity of which he himself, his writing duties, his rest and the turbine plotters are parts. By 'culture' I do not mean any machine symbolism, but a balanced mentality arising from work, its organization and a relaxed everyday life in which irrelevant points only produce a comic effect."

It is not by chance that the word organic is used twice in the passage I quote. It is not necessarily the word used by Aalto as a term. He is merely trying to describe the internal unity of his vision. A "balanced state of mind" is attainable in a "minimal existence". This may have been the way Aalto thought about small homes after the CIAM (Congrès International de l'Archi-

Artek

Exhibition of Aalto furniture at the Fortnum & Mason department store, London, 1933.

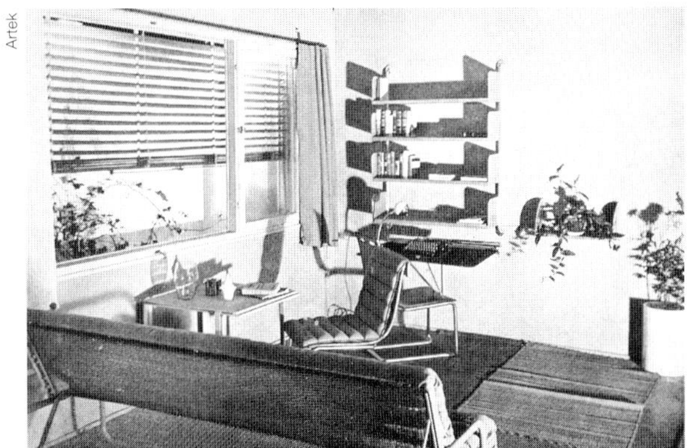
Artek

Housing Exhibition, Kunsthalle Helsinki, 1930.

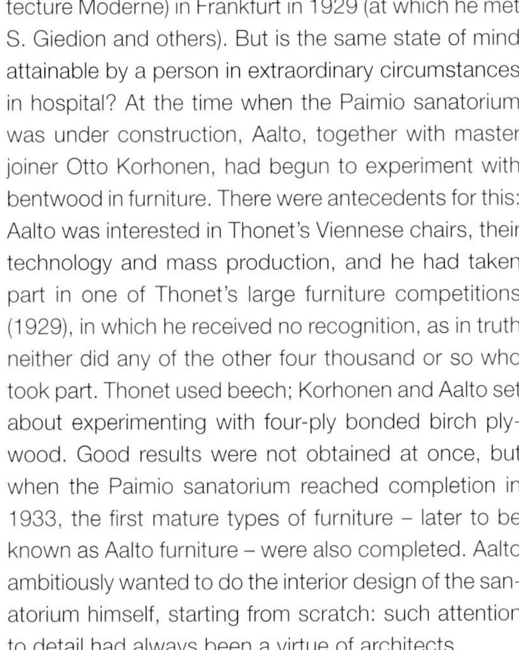

tecture Moderne) in Frankfurt in 1929 (at which he met S. Giedion and others). But is the same state of mind attainable by a person in extraordinary circumstances in hospital? At the time when the Paimio sanatorium was under construction, Aalto, together with master joiner Otto Korhonen, had begun to experiment with bentwood in furniture. There were antecedents for this: Aalto was interested in Thonet's Viennese chairs, their technology and mass production, and he had taken part in one of Thonet's large furniture competitions (1929), in which he received no recognition, as in truth neither did any of the other four thousand or so who took part. Thonet used beech; Korhonen and Aalto set about experimenting with four-ply bonded birch plywood. Good results were not obtained at once, but when the Paimio sanatorium reached completion in 1933, the first mature types of furniture – later to be known as Aalto furniture – were also completed. Aalto ambitiously wanted to do the interior design of the sanatorium himself, starting from scratch: such attention to detail had always been a virtue of architects.

Wood as a material and bent shapes together indicate something warm and easy to touch, something that in its tactility, its emotional and historical aspects has been with humankind a long time and can be trusted immediately, and has a familiar feel. The psychology of Aalto furniture –Aalto referred during the Paimio period specifically to the mental effect of furniture and fittings – appears clear-cut in this connection, although the question is ultimately one of complex contexts. It is easier for a practical design historian to follow what images of the furniture were created for the international public. The medium was in most cases an exhibition, not in Stockholm, where Aalto would no doubt have been pleased to unveil his achievements, and not in the Wohnbedarf shop of his kindred spirit S. Giedion in Switzerland, but in the exclusive Fortnum & Mason's department store in London. The idea was largely put forward by P. Morton Shand, who had met Aalto at the CIAM. Shand was a versatile writer, a fairly typical Oxonian who was an enthusiast of architecture and French wines.

In her study *The Reception and Criticism of Alvar Aalto in Britain*, Laura Iloniemi showed that Aalto had in mind a purely architectural exhibition as late as September 1933, but Shand and John Betjeman, who worked in the sphere of *The Architectural Review* and promoted the idea of the exhibition in London, urged Aalto to "humanize" the exhibition – i.e., to bring into it more furniture that would be understood by the average British socialite lady, who was not expected to be very aesthetically enlightened. This, it was felt, would give the exhibition a chance of success. Shand believed other suitable "humanizing" items could be carpets, textiles, ceramics and household ware. These groups of objects pointed towards the practical side of the Artek company which was founded two years later. Another of Artek's starting points was no doubt Giedion's Wohnbedarf.

In 1933, the United Kingdom was Finland's biggest export market and Europe's richest territory in terms of gross domestic product. Shand associated Aalto's furniture with trade and presented it as a refined product of the wood-processing industry. He emphasized the skills required, the comfort and light weight of the furniture and its low price. The exhibition was a success in spite of the fact that blond wood was and still is unusual in English décor. Shand declared to the press that the British would accept unusual shapes if they were convinced the chair was comfortable. This exhibition strengthened the polarization that was believed to exist between steel-tube and Aalto furniture. Aalto's wooden chairs won at least a round in London in 1933 and the general public was offered an interesting alternative. In the same year Finland took part in the Milan Triennale for the first time, once again displaying Aalto furniture. This was awarded a medal and Finland did well in other respects too. Three years

The Finland pavilion at the Milan Triennial, 1933.

later, at the sixth Triennale, after Artek had gone into business, Aino Aalto designed the Finnish section and she arranged it together with Nils-Gustav Hahl, the first managing director of Artek: in effect, it was an Artek exhibition stand. It was given suitable recognition, and this continued at the Paris Exhibition of 1937. Finland then had the first pavilion of its own since the 1900 exhibition, and the Aalto office was commissioned to design it after winning the competition for this. The pavilion featured a new tea trolley and glasses by both Aaltos. The most successful appearance on the global stage by Finland before the war – once again due to the Aaltos – was the New York World Fair: in the competition for the pavilion, both the Aalto office and Aino on her own had achieved a crushing hat-trick. The result was another 'symphony of wood'. Le Corbusier had already praised the wood theme of the Aaltos' pavilion in Paris: "Wood is the friend of mankind, pleasant to the touch and beautiful to look at, natural, full of imagination."

Although everything that the architectural firm of Alvar Aalto did was easily credited to the man himself, Aino Aalto also evinced a character of her own, though overshadowed by the extrovert Alvar. Aino Aalto (1894–1949) was an architect with a practical bent, who had practised making chairs and tables in a furniture factory. In 1922 her furnishings were the first prize in a lottery held by the Finnish Society of Crafts and Design; they have been characterized as 'English' in spirit. The ideology of functionalism fitted in well with her work; for the Minimum apartment exhibition of 1930 she designed a kitchen. From the viewpoint of Artek's image, what was important was her glassware. The Karhula and Iittala glassworks held a competition in 1932 with the aim of creating new table glassware and pressed-glass sets. The entry entitled 'Bölgeblick', which turned out to be by Aino Aalto, took second prize. The set, which comprised a tumbler, a jug, a sugar bowl and a cream jug, with assorted dishes and bowls, was serially produced under the name *Aalto* after further development. The set became one of the most successful and it has been constantly brought back into production. The stepped relief of this pressed glass was not an entirely unique invention, but Aino Aalto used it to make a coherent tableware set. As Timo Keinänen described it: "The plates, bowls and glasses have been designed in such a way that they can be used together. For example, the plates can be used as saucers under bowls. The proportions are such that the objects can conveniently be nested together or stacked to fit into a small space." The small home, interest in minimal existence, stackability, standardization, coherence, simplicity, sociality – the same interests of the new age embraced the whole of interior design and in general the issues of modern home life. These themes also gave Artek the integrated aspect through which it was viewed by the enlightened public and which gave continuity to its image. But Artek's policy was more than just a matter-of-fact continuance of Bauhaus: it had other dimensions. These arose from differences of temperament: if we consider Aino Aalto as a realist, Alvar could be described as almost a romantic. In this way they also complemented each other. When they both took part in a new glassware competition held by Karhula and Iittala in 1937, their entries differed in a characteristic way. As Timo Keinänen put it: "Whereas Alvar Aalto's entry, *The Eskimo Woman's Leather Breeches*, was as spontaneous as its name suggested, Aino's *Maija* (designs for charcuterie plates, cheese-and-biscuit plates, a bonbon bowl and a candleholder) were consummately thought through, polished and drawn with great precision. While Aalto's entry included disconnected fantasy vases [the Savoy vase, later known as the Aalto vase], Aino's proposal stuck closely to everyday needs in line with the principles of functionalism. Regrettably, only a part of Aino Aalto's proposals were put into practice, because in all their everyday nature they embodied in a pure form the goals by which functionalists sought to create a good and functional home environment for all classes of society." Within the sphere of Artek, this became particularly Aino Aalto's policy.

On 15 October 1935, a contract establishing Artek was signed by Aino and Alvar Aalto, Maire Gullichsen and Nils-Gustav Hahl. The name Artek carries an echo of 1920s rationalism: Walter Gropius declared the theme of the first Bauhaus exhibition in Weimar in 1923 to be 'art and technology, a new unity'. Nils-Gustav Hahl was an art researcher with an interest in architecture, design and cinema. Maire Gullichsen's field was primarily modern art, although she later showed an interest in glass design. Her activities within Artek included arranging modern art exhibitions: Artek may well be called a pioneer in this sphere as well. Art by Léger and Calder was displayed in the Artek shop in 1937 and there was a major exhibition of French contemporary art at Helsinki Art Hall in 1939. In the same year an initiative by Maire Gullichsen led to the start of a contemporary art association which, after the war, took over the management of the modern art exhibitions begun under the aegis of Artek.

The early ideology of Artek is described by what was known as the 'catechism', evidently written by Alvar Aalto and Nils-Gustav Hahl. It enumerates the fields in which Artek was to operate and the goals it should promote. Under the name Artek the first enumerators are the words *modern art, industry, interior design, propaganda* (the word 'publishing' had been crossed out and replaced with a then-fashionable term). Hahl wrote a short article about Artek in *Arkkitehti* magazine the first spring, in which he described Artek's mission as 'propagandizing on behalf of rational housing and interior design – as a financially independent body, Artek is closely linked in terms of principles with a ring of international enterprises possessing similar agendas'. According to the Artek team, paramount among the other parts of the ring were Wohnbedarf in Switzerland and Stylclair in Paris. The 'catechism' embodies a great deal of idealism, but Artek proved that it was practicable in part even in the small-scale circumstances of Finland. Artek succeeded in proving that 'healthy principles, open-minded clarity, technical logic' – concepts that were natural to functionalism – could be combined with the overarching human concepts of 'comfort and aesthetic quality'.

Iittala

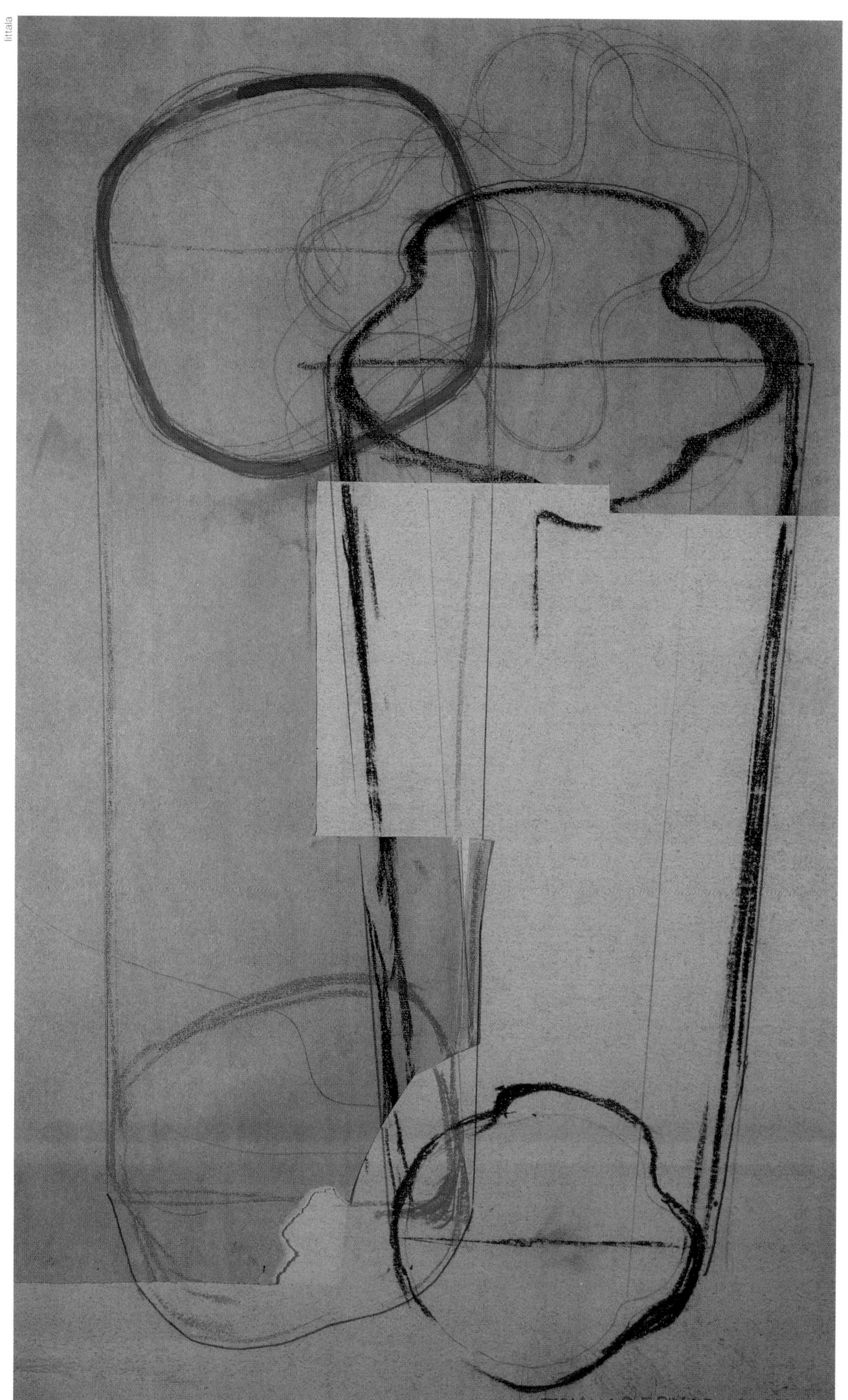

Alvar Aalto's entry entitled An Eskimo Woman's Leather Breeches *for the Karhula-Iittala glassworks competition for the Paris Universal Exhibition 1936. Aalto won the first prize. The vase was known as the Savoy vase (also Aalto vase).*

▶▶ *A pressed glass series designed by Aino Aalto for Iittala in 1933 won a prize in Milan in 1936. She originally won second prize in the competition under the name* Bölgeblick *in the Karhula-Iittala glassworks competition.*

The Influence of Functionalism on Alvar Aalto's Light Fittings

Markku Norvasuo

▶ *Light fitting for the conference room of the National Pensions Institute (1953–57). The brass (or occasionally gilded) metal finish that Aalto favoured gives added colour to the already warm glow of the incandescent bulb.*

Alvar Aalto's light fittings fall into three broad categories: the classicism of the 1920s, the period of functionalism (that started around 1928) and a final phase that began towards the end of the 1930s. The earliest light fitting to appear in his drawings was part of the furnishing for a bedroom designed in 1924. The early period also includes the light fittings for the Jyväskylä Workers' Club, the Hämäläinen Student Union Building and the Seinäjoki Defence Corps Building. Their idiom is typically underpinned by the theme of plants. He also designed candelabra and chandeliers for the churches restored then, but overall his work during that period was quite limited.

Towards the end of the 1920s he produced considerably more light fittings. The shift from neoclassicism to functionalism was pronounced and resulted in intensive experimentation with different modes and forms of lighting. From this point onwards Alvar Aalto and Aino Marsio-Aalto's office continuously designed light fittings. Aino Aalto died in 1949, but after her death a community of designers of Artek (founded in 1935) was involved in the interior design for numerous buildings from the 1950s onwards.

The impact of such collaboration on Aalto's designs is a salient puzzle, but one that is difficult to study and which nevertheless affects his other works, not least the buildings themselves. Another relevant issue here is the chronological development of Aalto's light fittings, but that is easier to approach by studying the designs.

The genuine interest that the functionalists had for technical solutions is also reflected in Aalto's light fittings. It was typical for Aalto to consider several aspects simultaneously, particularly lighting and acoustics, by applying the same ideas for a solution. Many of the ideas flowing through his mind overlapped, and were perhaps rejected, only to reappear subsequently in another form. This process appears to have continued right up to his late works.

Functionalism coincided with an important stage in the development of the electric light in the Nordic countries. The use of electricity was rapidly becoming widespread. The power plant at Imatra was commissioned in 1928, the transmission grid expanded and the production of light bulbs started in Finland. The ordinary incandescent bulb took on its present shape in the beginning of the 1930s. Methods for calculating lighting were established to control the technology. Two organizations were founded in Sweden, Ljuskultur and FERA, to promote the sensible use of light. The new opportunities that electric lighting offered were demonstrated in a wide range of projects and exhibitions. Lighting was prominently displayed in the 1930 Stockholm Exposition, an important milestone in Swedish functionalism. It featured an 80-metre high advertising tower illuminated by thousands of lamps, floodlights and luminous opal glass surfaces. Opal glass enhanced for use in lighting, with flat surfaces and spherical canopies, became one of the characteristics of functionalism.

The Southwestern Finland Agricultural Cooperative Building represented a breakthrough in the use of electric lighting in Aalto's works. As a building it did not herald a new style, but the modern age for lighting had dawned. The plans contain different drawings for some 15 types of light fittings. Their very diversity catches the attention. There were different models especially for the dressing room mirror, the music stand, the programme board and the ticket office, and light fittings were also designed for the stairs, the wall of the restaurant and for lighting the façade. Signs with background lighting and tubular lighting between the cornice strips and ceiling were designed for the Jyväskylä Defence Corps Building at around the same time (1926–29). Standardized furnishing was also a part of functionalism. Poul Henningsen's PH light fitting was used in the Jyväskylä Defence Corps Building, the Agricultural Cooperative Building and the Turun Sanomat

Alvar Aalto Archives

The ceiling light of the Turun Sanomat newspaper offices (1928–30), which presaged the stylistic idiom of the fluorescent light. The ceilings were grooved for the wiring.

newspaper offices. Most of the light fittings for the latter locations, however, were designed by Aalto himself. Aalto also used a free hand with PH light fittings; for instance, countersinking them into the ceilings. One of the drawings for the Turun Sanomat newspaper offices shows how Aalto replaced an original PH light fitting with his own solution based on it. At that time Aalto's drawings for light fittings typically contained the marking "STANDARD No......" New designs were so frequent, however, that in practice Aalto's own 'standards' had little impact. A set of drawings for 'standard furniture' date from the period 1929–32. They include Aalto's own light fittings as well as the standard light fittings and accessories of the time.

A basic feature of the PH light fitting was its slat construction. Henningsen was interested in the ideal light fitting and analysed the standard constructions of the period to find a basis for it. The main issue was how to make an effective light fitting with matt or diffusive surfaces that directed the light in the direction desired. These reflecting surfaces of the PH light fitting were Henningsen's solution to this problem.

Some interesting drafts can be found in the drawings for the Agricultural Cooperative Building that obviously aimed to resolve the same problem by using reflecting surfaces for the lighting in the ceiling elements of the entrance hall of the theatre. The drafts probably date from 1927 or 1928. Aalto was working on issues of acoustics at that time, and developed a similar solution based on laminations for those also. Henningsen's influence in this experimentation can only be surmised. Despite that, the final result did not incorporate lamellas; instead, the unmodified lamp was placed under the edge of the element.

This reveals the excitement and division within the functional movement. A rational function does not automatically produce its own form, while on the other hand the inherent perspective of the form makes the functions relative. Aalto realized the functional importance of the slat structure and started working to incorporate them in the latticework of building façades and as acoustic cladding for interior walls in the 1930s. Nevertheless, his search for form in his designs for light fittings initially led to other types of solutions. Aalto seems to have looked in vain for an aesthetically pleasing interpretation of a design based on Henningsen's technique. It was not perhaps until the 1950s that his work with reflecting slats bore fruit with the idea of using them as sculptural elements. The lighting techniques of the lamp stands from that period are good. Conversely, *Beehive* is an excellent example from the early 1950s of how the 'function' of slats has become purely aesthetic. The idea for the shape, closely resembling a light fitting, had appeared before functionalism in the décor of the café in the Jyväskylä Defence Corps Building.

All Aalto's main functional works were important from the standpoint of light fittings: the Turun Sanomat newspaper offices (1928–30); the Paimio Tuberculosis Sanatorium (1929–32), and Viipuri Library (1927–33). Not many light fittings were designed for Viipuri Library. However, light fittings of the 1933 version splendidly demonstrated functional design ideals. Those light fittings included spotlights on rails in the newspaper reading room and wall washers sunk into the ceiling of the large lending room that illuminated the wall surfaces. Both forms of lighting are widely used today. Aalto's office also attempted to compute the dimensioning for the arrangement of ceiling reflectors and gave coordinates to the location of light fittings in the reference room. The light fittings designed for the building were austere compared to Aalto's later libraries.

Aalto appears to have applied all possible ideas for form and function for his light fittings throughout the 1920s and '30s. That was an extremely productive period for the design of light fittings and emphasized their functional properties. A lighting set from the Turun Sanomat newspaper offices, for instance, 'recycled' the light from within the glass door of a display case to illuminate the space below as well. Other results of Aalto's experimentation with laminations were a round weather vane light fitting and an elongated light fitting for the ceiling of the corridor. The laminated con-

Alvar Aalto Archives/Simo Rista

A triple-domed standard lamp, nicknamed Angel *(Artek model A 809), was designed in 1959 for La Maison Louis Carré. The picture shows a modified version from Finlandia Hall. The dome is a mature application of Aalto's slat concept.*

Artek

Artek

Artek

Artek

Artek

a b c
d e
Examples of Aalto's variations on a theme in the 1950s. in order, Artek models A 605, A 337 (Flying Saucer), A 110 (Hand Grenade), A 624 *and* A 604. *The brass glare shield (pictures c and e) came into use in the early 1950s.*

Alvar Aalto Archives/Gustaf Welin

The easily cleaned, glass-domed light fittings of the glass stairway and hall of Viipuri Library (1933–35) fulfilled the ideals of functionalism. In the picture from the right are Aino and Alvar Aalto with Aarne Ervi.

struction used in the latter was a forerunner to the fluorescent lamps typical nowadays. Possibly Aalto's inquisitive experimentation with all types of ideas is the reason why many of his light fittings seemed to anticipate solutions that were later widely adopted. The fluorescent lamp was not introduced until the 1940s.

A special feature of the Paimio Tuberculosis Sanatorium is the reflector, which Aalto later applied in much of his outdoor column lighting. The original shape of the light fitting comes from the Paimio Tuberculosis Sanatorium. Aalto used the same principle in the light fitting for the sickroom. These light fittings represent an extremely indirect method of lighting compared to Aalto's other work. The lamps in later column lighting were no longer hidden from sight and the reflector visor was of less importance to the illumination.

The importance of reflectors is also manifest from the dark colouring of the ceiling of the sanatorium's sickroom and the bevelled bottom part of the window wall. Aalto has clearly focused on what the observer sees around him. The wall surfaces in Paimio are crucial. Later it was the individuality of the light fitting that was emphasized. The functionalist opal sphere had quite a bright and uninteresting surface, although the opal glass effectively eliminated glare. Aalto used sandblasted glass and opal glass more abundantly during the functionalist period than later. In his newer light fittings, which were mostly made of metal, the visual solution called for a compromise in efficacy. The construction of the light fitting, through which the light was filtered, was emphasized to counterbalance this compromise. He started this approach at the end of the 1930s in the furnishing of the Savoy Restaurant (which included the brass 'Golden Bell' from 1937) while simultaneously working towards using light with a warmer quality.

Although the light fittings from the functionalist period stand out from Aalto's other works, they are clearly linked to his later work in many ways. Firstly, Aalto generally opted for the stylish use of light. He paid great attention to the glare shield in many of the light fittings of that period (as he did in the skylights of the Viipuri Library). Secondly, they formed the basis for a very diversified range of light fittings and for ideas on the use of light. Thirdly, they produced many themes for shape, such as slats and various reflectors. And finally, it can be seen that the raw ideal of rational design was not fully applied to many light fittings. An extra dimension is retained: let's call it striving towards a warmer, cosier end result.

The maturity of the solutions combined with the volume and consistency of output makes the 1950s the high point in Aalto's design of light fittings. In its abundance and diversity of ideas, however, the func-

Design Forum Finland/Rauno Träskelin

The lobby of Finlandia Hall (completed 1975). In front of the windows are tripartite light fittings with sandblasted surfaces facing outwards. In the evening, the light is reflected from the window panes.

tionalist period was not left behind and forms an important underpinning for later light fitting designs. The period from the end of the 1930s to the beginning of the 1950s seems of lesser importance, probably due to the large role that designing industrial, residential and communal buildings played. After that, public construction again increased and remained at a high level through the 1960s and '70s.

A distinct feature of the light fittings from the 1950s is the deliberate variation of materials, shapes and parts, which could also be called the aesthetics of interchanging, adding and combining. By modifying some parts of a light fitting, different models of a fitting could be created for different environments and purposes. The methodology of such modification was to a large extent related to the contextual principles of classicism. As well as this classical approach, the organic and ornamental content that preceded functionalism (and it was partly retained during it) returned to Aalto's light fittings.

The light fittings in the National Pensions Institute (1953–1957) offer good examples. Aalto used the same brass canopy in two ceiling lights (in one he added a reflector), and in a lamp stand while tripling it in the 'chandelier' for the lobby and doubling it for the table lamp in the library. The materials were also changed: bright, patinated brass and white paint refined the appearance of the lamps to suit the room, although the canopy remained almost unchanged. An interesting coordination was also created between the board's conference room and the personnel's restaurant, where the same corresponding elements gave the room atmosphere. The wooden latticework or enamelled heating elements on the ceilings, the fabric covering or glazed tiling of the walls, and the light fittings of brass or opal glass with white details made the conference room festive and the restaurant cosy.

The brass light fitting in the conference room of the National Pensions Institute, in particular, has been compared to an oil lamp, which also symbolized Aalto's aim of using warm shades of light. Similarly, the stems of the light fittings are reminiscent of sunlight filtered through branches or a grove of birch trees. Such metaphors, especially as the premise for design, are difficult to ascertain later. Nevertheless, the drafts for the Southwestern Finland Agricultural Cooperative Building contained a sketch of an oil lamp with glass and metal ornamentation, and variations on the theme for a bracket lamp. In retrospect, the Agricultural Cooperative Building does seem to be a crucial work that anticipated various aspects of Aalto's light fittings. The romantic idea of warm filtered light, distinct classical context and functional convenience characterize these dimensions very well.

Out into the World

Design, Industry and Internationalization in the 1950s and '60s

Pekka Korvenmaa

The international success of Finnish design and applied arts had its basis in the post-war years of shortages and austerity and its heyday lasted from the early 1950s to the end of the following decade. Also known as the "Golden Age", this period is often compared to the similarly termed turn of the 19th and 20th centuries, when Finnish architecture and applied arts were also the focus of international attention. In both periods, praise from abroad raised and enhanced the status and importance of these fields and their leading names in the domestic context. Unlike the turn of the past century, the period discussed below mostly involved the actual industrialization of design in Finland. This emphasis is present despite the fact that the image of post-war success in Finnish design is mainly associated with crafted artefacts or objects made in small series that were identified as art.

Museum of Art and Design

The Finland pavilion at the Milan Triennial of 1954, exhibition design by Tapio Wirkkala.

▶▶ *Antti Nurmesniemi, Kettle, 1960s and 1970s, Wärstilä Ltd.*

Like the nation's economy and cultural sector, design and applied arts in Finland entered the post-war era from scratch in a situation severely limited by severe peace terms and war reparations to the Soviet Union. But this situation also permited the realization of skills deriving from the pre-war years. Kaj Franck, Gunnel Nyman, Lisa Johansson-Pape, Maija Heikinheimo, Ilmari Tapiovaara, among other designers, had studied and partly trained for their professions before the second world war. They had also adopted the egalitarian views implicit in Functionalism, the Nordic Modernism of the period. There was now real demand for these values as an environment and a material culture was to be created with limited resources for as many as possible. Finland was still a predominantly rural society, whose industries mostly relied on the forest sector. The applied arts presented after the war in exhibitions to the public was mostly crafted ceramics, glass and textiles in the form of tapestries and *ryijy* (*rya*) rugs. Alongside these areas the industrial utilization of applied arts and design mainly took place in the furniture industry and in the household tableware produced by the Arabia factory. War reparations speeded the growth of the metal industry but a broader use of industrial design, and education in the field, did not begin until the industrial basis and the range of available materials started to grow in the late 1950s.

Finnish design in the 1950s should be discussed with reference not only to its brilliant success at the Milan Triennials in 1951, 1954 and 1957 but also with regard to how much Finnish homes and public facilities benefited from design expertise channelled into industry. The industrial connection is of prime importance, for only through it could the larger groups of domestic consumers be reached. For these buyers, exclusive applied arts objects or art glass made in small series played a secondary role to the basic needs of homes.

The Finnish Society of Crafts and Design and its leading figure, the energetic organizer and public-relations expert Herman Olof Gummerus arranged presentations of applied arts and design at the exhibitions created a comprehensive image of a synthesis of nature, creativity and originality. This synthesis was prominently characterized by markedly art-oriented design products and the designers themselves – Franck, Wirkkala, Sarpaneva – who were elevated by a skilled manipulation of their public image to Promethean dimensions, as the living instruments of a primal will of imbuing form. During the 1950s, the range of products on show in international exhibitions began to include growing numbers of serially manufactured products, particularly in glass, ceramics and furniture. The marketing of utility objects for the home was naturally promoted by the fact that their designers had already earned a name for themselves in creating applied arts artefacts for the elite, for example in free-form glass. Exports in fields utilizing design skills and expertise grew continuously during the 1950s and expanded markedly as a result of the EFTA agreement of 1961.

Accordingly, in the 1950s Finnish applied arts and design became international at two levels: in the sphere of public exposure and professional reputation, and in the actual export industries based on design. This was no insignificant achievement in view of Finland's modest economy, marginal geographical location and low degree of industrialization. Design also found support in a political trend that sought to make it clear to the international community that in terms of society and culture Finland belonged to the West, i.e. to the "Free World". It was no coincidence that the Scandinavian Design exhibition, which began its three-year tour of North America in 1954, coincided with the worst stage of the Cold War. It was extremely important for Finland to present itself in the same front as the Scandinavian democracies. There was a functioning symbiosis of foreign policy and design benefiting both parties. Achieving international attention and fame, Finnish design projected the image of a modern and creative society respecting the individual, while exports of design products gained market visibility with the means of foreign policy. Internationalization worked both ways. As Finnish design was presented and promoted abroad, its far-ranging "ambassadors" established contacts for importing the latest trends in design education and professional practices. Towards the close of the 1950s this led to the rapid modernization of the design community, involving the designers, their organizations, promotion, industry and marketing. Within a short time, this comprehensive project involving many parties had led to world fame, and even to a kind of position of authority. Although developments followed a different course than at the turn of the century when the arts and culture of the Grand Duchy of Finland were put on the international scene, the new situation also involved economic and cultural reconstruction in difficult conditions, battling against being set aside.

As industry made increasing use of design professionals, the domestic market, enjoying the benefits of protective tariffs, provided an opportunity to respond to demand fanned by a rising standard of living with Finnish-made products following the tenets of modernism, or at least adapted to its principles. Especially in ceramic tableware and furniture many products that had won international prizes now became available to middle-class consumers. This was by no means insignificant. In the United States and partly in Continental Europe, similar products were available only to the elite. It can be said that from the 1950s to the end of the 1960s a modernism of high international standard in architecture and design became established in the creation and formation of the environment in public contexts, and to a marked degree also in private milieus. The tableware, coffee-pots and chairs iconized in later writings and exhibitions belonged to the everyday environment of a large sector of the population – with more expensive glassware sold with the designer's name for special festive use.

High-standard expertise in design required a developed educational basis. Training and education in this field was concentrated in an institution founded in 1871 and known since 1949 as the Institute of Arts and Crafts. Already in the pre-war years it provided training for a broad professional field. One result of this was that, for example, like Kaj Franck many designers known for their work in glass and ceramics had originally graduated in other fields, such as textile design. After the second world war, design education underwent thorough reforms and was explicitly steered closer to industry and practical work, while its preparatory stages taught students a command of the general principles of colour, form and composition. As the industrial sector grew and diversified and the markets and demand grew during the 1950s, the educational system prepared a growing number of people with an increasingly higher level of training to meet these needs. For example, the growing corps of interior architects had a growing field of professional activity in both commercial construction and public building.

Design education, professional practice and industry utilizing it were all influenced by the rapid industrialization of the nation and on a more general level by the concept of industry basing on the achievements of technological progress as one of the main factors shaping modern society and culture.

In the mid-1950s the originally American concept

Museum of Art and Design/Pietinen

Richard Lindh, Solifer *moped, 1958, Wich Bensow/Solifer*

Tapio Wirkkala, Aslak *glassware, 1966 Iittala.*

Museum of Art and Design/Martti Ounamo

Museum of Art and Design/Otso Pietinen

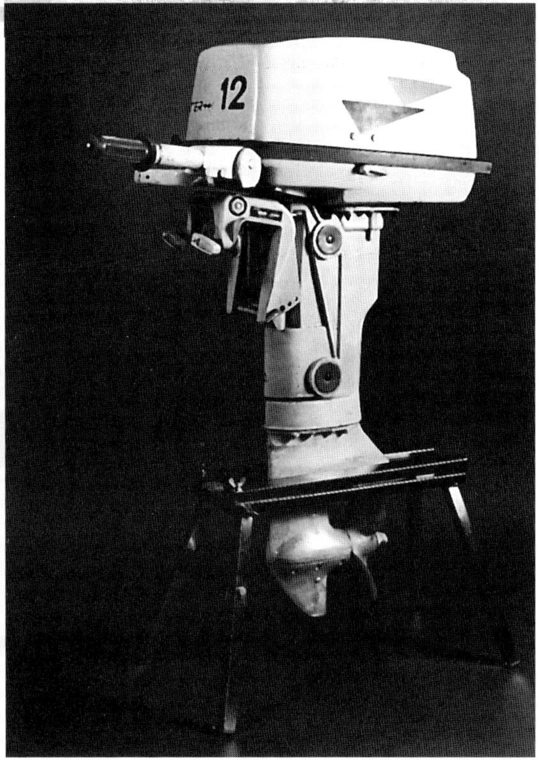

Museum of Art and Design/Aimo Hyvärinen

Jukka Pellinen, Outboard motor Terhi 12, *1964, Vacolet Oy.*

Ulla Procopé, Liekki *casseroles 1957, Arabia.*

of product design emerged in applied arts and design in Finland. Product design was no longer bound to the traditional material-based educational and professional image of the applied arts. In Finland, this conformed well to the diversification of industrial products and materials. As post-war rationing came to an end after the turn of the 1940s and '50s, tubular steel, for example, again became available to the furniture industry, which speeded the development of lightweight all-purpose chairs. The metal industry, which post-war reparations to the Soviet Union had forced to undergo transformation, began to employ designers for consumer goods, such as cast-iron kitchen utensils. An unprecedented rise in housing development and the standard of equipment of homes speeded the manufacture of kitchen appliances such as cookers and refrigerators, for which the contribution of designers was now needed. The plastics that had such impact on the culture of manufacture and consumption of the following decade were first adopted in the late 1950s by the furniture industry, followed by other consumer-goods industries. Foam rubber and the later expanded plastic that remained invisible in furniture revolutionized the design and manufacturing process with regard to padding and upholstery and partly also the framework. Form-cast polystyrene permitted a framework that was sculptural and anatomically correct, with the seat, back and arm-rest all made of one piece. Translucent and opal acrylates gave lamp designers opportunities not possible with metal or glass.

In the design profession these developments led to the emergence of industrial design as a separate sector of activity and, before long, education. Professional designers had worked for industry all along, but basing their work on specific materials. The new situation, however, involved general product, equipment and environmental design and the management of a designed corporate image, within which design skills came to be redefined. Finnish developments were attuned to the international scene. Particularly in the early 1960s there was extensive discussion on the role of industrial design within the International Council of Societies of Industrial Design. In Finland, the ORNAMO association for ornamental art renamed itself the Finnish Association of Designers ORNAMO in 1966. The year 1961 marked the introduction of industrial design as a subject at the Institute of Arts and Crafts. Around this time Finnish industry and its official organizations took a serious interest in the potential contribution of industrial design to the industrial life of the nation and as a factor for improving international competitiveness. In this way, the internationalization of design, launched in the early 1950s by a few leading companies, funded by them and the state and initially relying on the skills of H. O. Gummerus, began to achieve a broader perspective in terms of industrial and educational policy. As trade with the west grew in the early 1960s, exports of textiles and furniture began to have a definite significance for the economy. In this respect, the early 1960s reaped the benefits of the efforts of the previous decade. The international renown that had thus been achieved was utilized and developed further through active marketing efforts and the collaboration of industry and designers. The officially protected domestic market, in turn, ensured steady demand.

From the 1950s the domestic public image of design, bolstered by international repute, markedly focused on individuals whereby the marketed products were associated with the artistic aura of famous names in design. As developments increasingly led towards serial manufacture, an expanding range of consumer goods and appliances, it no longer seemed sensible to define the authorship and marketing aspects of a product around the contribution of the individual designers. These considerations had figured in international discussion and debate but had been overshadowed by the focus on the individual in Finnish design. They were, however, formulated by Kaj Franck in 1965 in his well-known statement on behalf of anonymity in the marketing of serially manufactured products. In the debates of the late 1960s Franck's arguments were adopted by a new generation of designers who had grown up in an industrialized welfare state and whose attitudes were, from the outset, international, global, and radical. The art oriented and individualistic presentation of Finnish design at Expo 67 in Montreal provoked a great deal of criticism, prompting a changing of perspective away from the designer and from individual objects. In these years, the field of industrial design and the design of objects in general expanded into general product and environmental design, which included, among other things, the working environment, traffic and urban space. Students adopted the concept of ecological and social responsibility to be taken by design and those utilizing it. The strong artist identity of design professionals, which industry had promoted, now began to break down as the requirements of industry and the ideological climate changed. This phenomenon was not unique in Finland, or internationally: it involved the emergence of the post-war baby boom generation of new participants and actors who questioned the leading figures who had been in power since the second world war. For example in architecture the young generation of these years emphasized generalization, prefabrication and a blurring of the formerly so prominent individual designer.

Although debate on design, its specific responsibilities and the role of the individual designer took on radical overtones and became heated towards the close of the 1960s, the design community, industry and exporters cooperated well. The industrial applications of design had continued to expand, resulting in growing exports in the fields and sectors concerned. A number of textile and garment firms, most notably Marimekko, based their whole success on innovative product development and marketing. In materials, for example, the command of hardened plastics in furniture making combined with high-standard design had also led to international fame and the markets. Finnish industry still had the daring to invest in bold design, as developments of the past years had proven such design to be profitable. The foundation that had been laid after the second world war and the concerted effort of several parties still provided a basis of support for design both in Finland and abroad. During these years Finland had developed from a predominantly agrarian, outlying and poor nation in the margins of Europe into an industrialized welfare state with a high standard of living with active international contacts. Within this broader context of developments, the opportunities of design had been applied boldly to the benefit of design professionals and industry, and, indirectly, for the good of the nation as a whole.

Museum of Art and Design

Ilmari Tapiovaara, Lukki *series of chairs, 1950–54*

Modern Glass Design

Artists and Designers

Tuula Poutasuo

Motto:
"If one has held in one's hand a piece of translucent amber with an insect trapped in it thousands of years ago when it was still resin, one may also appreciate the fascinating mystique of glass. One will see glass as the result of the play of light and instantaneous solidification of molten material, the fruit of forces of nature commanded on impulse to stop and stand still for eternity."
Gunnel Nyman 1948

Museum of Art and Design

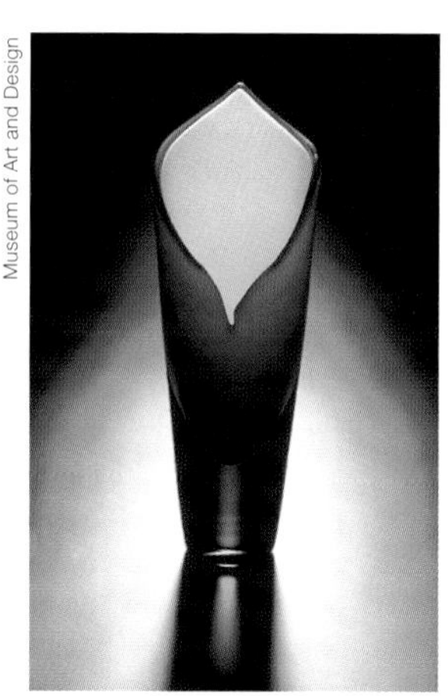

Gunnel Nyman, Calla *vase, 1946. Free blown green glass, opal inside. Height 32,5 cm. Riihimäen Lasi, Riihimäki.*

▶ *Gunnel Nyman,* Serpentine *vase, 1947. Free blown clear crystal, inside the vase is a filigree-ribbon-spiral. Height 34 cm. Nuutajärven Lasi, Nuutajärvi.*

Gunnel Nyman
1909–1948

Gunnel Nyman's unique, lyrical and beautiful work in glass was renowned throughout the Nordic countries in her last years. Her *Calla* and *Serpentine* vases, *Fasetti* bowls and bubble glass were all avant-garde creations in their day. The *Fasetti* bowls, designed during the second world war, were solely intended as art objects, and they marked the beginning of purely sculptural approach in Nyman's oeuvre. The *Calla* vase, a stylized calla lily shape, is particularly sculptural in form. Nyman's best-known utility objects are her bubble-glass jugs, tumblers, sugar bowls and creamers.

This much-admired designer followed a singularly consistent line of clarity, simple form and fluid sculptural properties all enhanced and reinforced by thick glass. The vases often entail a fascinating tension of strength and poetry, with the inner surface marked by a network of air bubble resembling dewdrops, a veil of colour, or a "floating streamer".

Gunnel Nyman originally designed for various glassworks – for Nuutajärvi for the last two years of her life. There she began to work together with the glassblowers, which was something new, especially for women designers. This was an opportunity to experiment and to study the possibilities of glass. The beautiful and praised designs that were thus created marked a new course for the old glassworks. Gunnel Nyman was originally an interior designer who was also successful in furniture and silver design. Her art glass and furniture designs were awarded gold and silver medals at the Paris World Fair in 1937, and she received a posthumous gold medal at the Milan Triennial of 1951.

A memorial collection of designs by Gunnel Nyman was on show at the Finnish Applied Arts exhibition of 1948. In his review of the exhibition, Kaj Franck noted: "Gunnel Nyman is no longer with us. But her works in glass – some clear like crystallized thought, some softly glowing as if they had captured something of their maker's essence in the moment of being created – were the most profound experiences of the whole show. Her works are a legacy for our young art of glass design, and for the nation's applied arts as a whole."

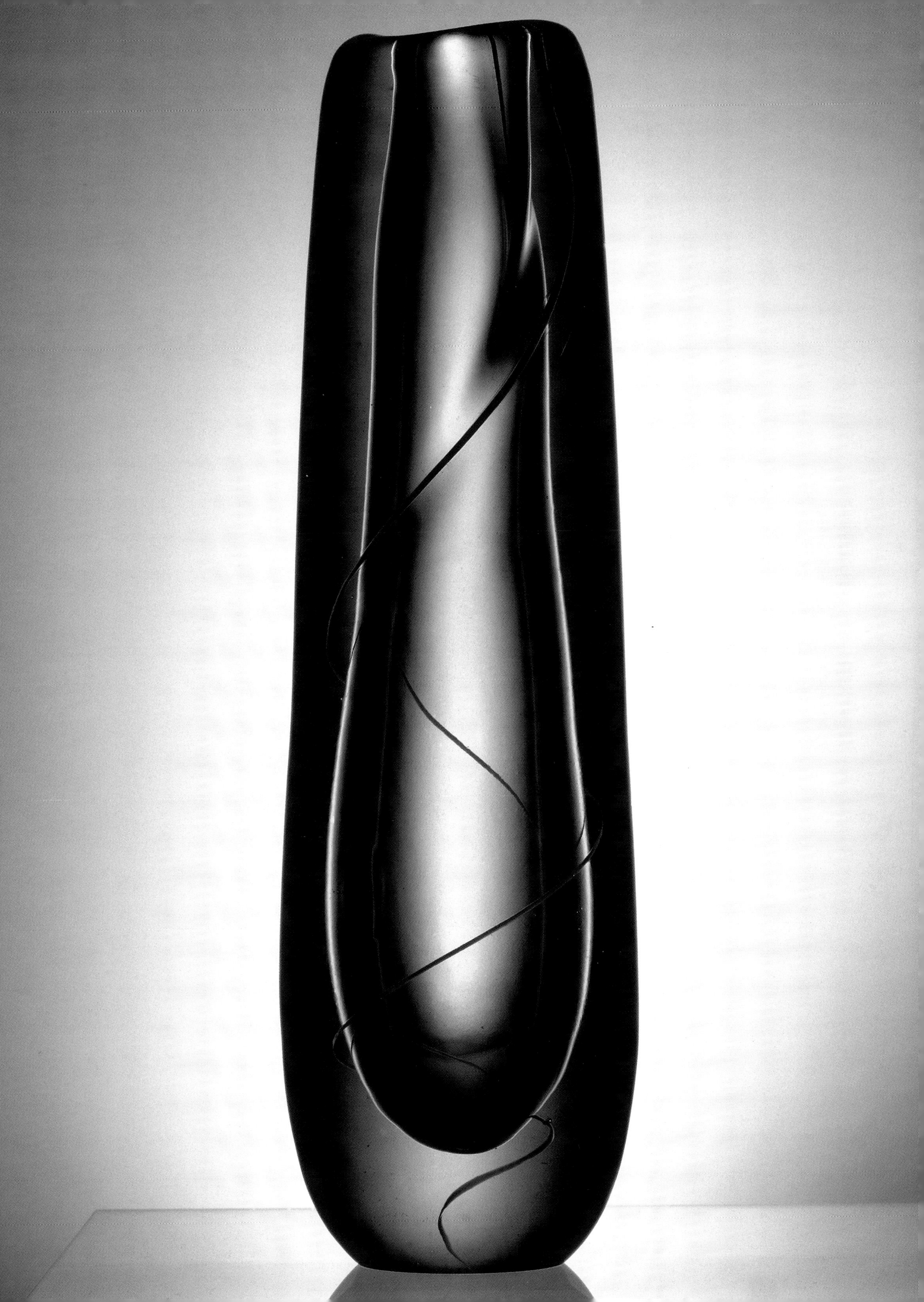

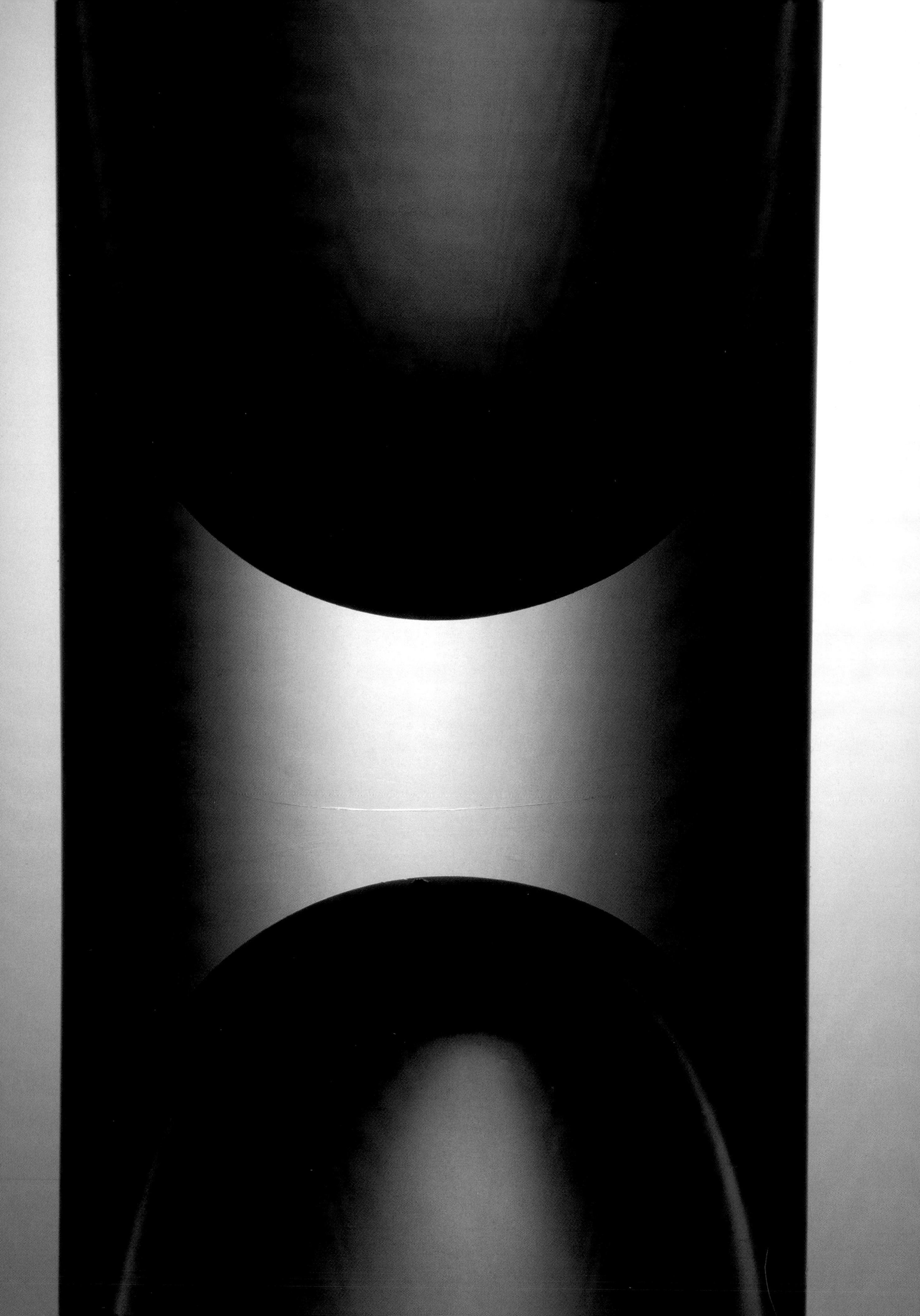

Tapio Wirkkala
1915–1985

Tapio Wirkkala's large *Jäävuori* (Iceberg) vase is a suggestive object from the 1950s. This free-form crystal piece stands on a pedestal at the Finnish Glass Museum and is an expression of creative energy. With its sharply cut "precipices" it appears to be in continuous movement. Wirkkala approached glass like the material of a sculptor. At the same time he was involved in making free-form wooden works of sculpture from aircraft plywood. Along with bowls and vases of reduced plastic form, the expressionistic "ice sculptures" belonged to the glass collection by Wirkkala which won the Grand Prix at the Milan Triennial in 1951. The works were regarded as brilliant expressions of the exoticism of the North. This expressive glass sculpture, however, was ahead of its time, and a refined clear-cut style was chosen to represent Finland. Free form and expressiveness reappeared in Wirkkala's *Paadarin jäät* (Paadar's ice) glass pieces at the 1960 triennial. The surface of the cast abstract pieces was marked with a graphic pattern of grooves, prefiguring the free trends of the new decade.

Tapio Wirkkala has said that "a designer must have eyes in his fingertips". In 1946, when he became a designer at Iittala after winning a design competition for engraved glass, he began to participate in the actual glass-making process, studying his material thoroughly from the making of moulds to the blowing stage. A designer like this was something new, and the glassmakers were not all that pleased at first. But Wirkkala was accepted after he had engraved 30 of his own shell-shaped bowls. He was skilled with his hands and an excellent draughtsman. His drawing skills can be seen in the figurative motifs of his early art glass. Wirkkala's best-known early works are his leaf and shell-shaped bowls and his *Kantarelli* (Chanterelle) vase. These are sculptural objects of reduced and clarified form.

◀ *Tapio Wirkkala: Vase, 1955. Mould and steam blown. Coloured interior casing. Hight 20–34 cm. Iittala Glassworks, Iittala.*

▶ *Tapio Wirkkala's* Chanterelle *vase, 1946. Mould blown. Height 15–19 cm. Iittala Glassworks, Iittala.*

Maaria Wirkkala/Pirjo Honkasalo

Tapio Wirkkala

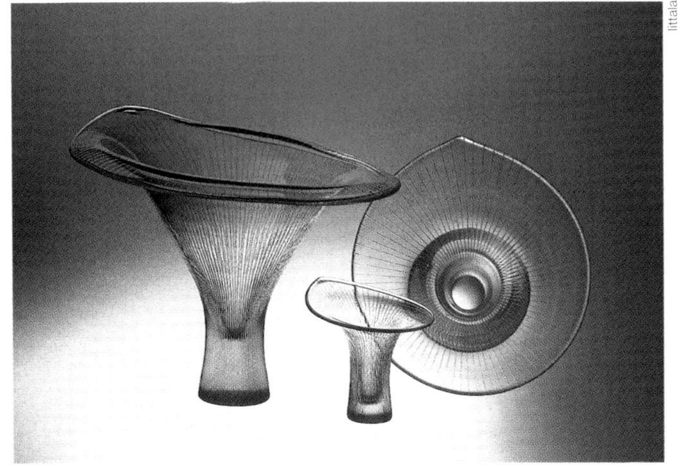
Iittala

Design Forum Finland/Rauno Träskelin

Tapio Wirkkala, Linssi *bowl, 1980, unique piece. Centrifugal cast. Height 10,7 cm, diameter 35 cm. Iittala Glassworks, Iittala.*

Wirkkala was also interested in the abstract and geometric forms of nature. The camera was an important tool with which he recorded the details of nature from plants and small creatures to whirlpools and the surface structures of the soil. Their influence, however, is mostly discernible as a certain mood in many of his works.

The optics of glass were also of interest to Wirkkala. The refractive properties of glass came into their own in clear-cut pieces made of thick glass. Among the earliest examples of Wirkkala's study of glass optics are his clear-glass comb-cut vases of the 1940s and '50s and glass pieces with a bubble of air inside. The discrepancies of exterior and interior form will also enhance the optic properties of glass. Also in the *Tapio* glasses, from 1952, there is a bubble in the conical stem and the carafe stopper. The large and thick-rimmed *Linssi* (Lens) bowl from 1980 is also an interesting design. Wirkkala's daughter Maaria mentions that the bowl clearly refers to her late father's interest in photography. The inner surface is completely straight, while the exterior protrudes markedly and curves inward. The rim acts like the lens of a camera. A coffee cup placed in the bowl is seen upside down through the lens, as is also the view opening from the window when seen through the lens.

Tapio Wirkkala designed many popular sets of glassware. Iittala still manufactures the *Tapio* series of the 1950s and the Ovalis vase, the *Ultima Thule* of the 1960s and *Gaissa* of the 1970s. The *Kantarelli* (Chanterelle) vase from 1946 is made as a series of art glass pieces.

In his Finnish works, Wirkkala preferred the clarity inherent to glass, but in the mid-1960s, when he was invited to design for Venini of Venice, he was introduced to the world of colour of Murano glass. Although Venini was famous for its colourful luxury objects, Wirkkala worked in more restrained hues that gave more expression to the limpidity and transparency of glass. Well-known designs by Wirkkala include the *Coreano* bowl and the *Bolla* bottles. The painterly *Coreano*, with a blue and a green spiral as in the waters of the rapids, especially appeals to Finnish friends of design.

Wirkkala was a versatile and gifted designer who was not restricted to glass. Already in the 1950s he designed silver objects for Kultakeskus, Finland's largest manufacturer of objects in precious metal, and china for Rosenthal of Germany. The 1960s included not only glass for Venini but also objects in various materials for Finnish manufacturers. Wirkkala's "popular items" include Finnish banknotes, which he redesigned in the late 1940s, the Finlandia vodka bottle, incandescent lamps, mustard-jar glasses and a plastic ketchup bottle. In the late 1950s plastic tableware designed by Wirkkala was used by the national airline, Finnair, in its then new Caravelle passenger jets. When Finnair began to fly passengers to North America in the late 1960s, food was served on Wirkkala's new plastic tableware and refreshments in his "ice-covered" *Ultima Thule* tumblers.

The hand of the designer is also evident in the Finnish Glass Museum at Riihimäki, installed in the old buildings of the Riihimäki Glassworks. Together with his son, interior architect Sami Wirkkala, Tapio Wirkkala designed the renovation of the building for its conversion into a museum as well as the permanent exhibition. The museum was opened to the public in 1981.

Tapio Wirkkala's oeuvre was extremely broad in scope. It required not only a great deal of creative energy but also considerable effort and extensive travel. The artist offset this way of life with long stays in Northern Lapland. Wirkkala in Lapland carving wooden birds or cups out of curly-grained wood is a Finnish legend.

Tapio Wirkkala,
Correano *plate, 1968.*
Blown. Diameter 60 cm.
Venini. Venice.

Timo Sarpaneva
1926–

On a beautiful late winter day the blinding ice of the Gulf of Finland can be seen from the windows of Timo Sarpaneva's studio in Helsinki's South Harbour. One could hardly imagine a better setting for his new sculptures in glass, which change with the light. The pieces glow in their intensive colours like immense jewels. Their varied and abstract world of colour is on continuous motion.

An amber-hued ellipse is like a window onto the sea, and *Fiery Gaze*, a group of sculptures, has a distinct appeal. The name refers to the eyes of the suffering Christ. Seen through the planes of colour, they seem to be moving like a continually changing landscape.

The new works of sculpture were created at Pino Signoretto's workshop at the glassworks island of Murano in Venice. Sarpaneva has designed glass for Venini of Murano since the 1970s.

"Venini is the only glassmaker in Venice that still knows the methods with which these works, and their world of colour, are mastered. Making them has been a long and inspiring creative process lasting several years. It was particularly difficult, and interesting, to design completely new colours for the pieces. With their thousands of hues, these are mysterious works. No other material gives such depth. Mysteriously mystical worlds can be embedded in glass."

Where do the ideas for the works come from? "Roaming the world, one must keep one's eyes and heart open to life, and new impulses. When I make works of glass sculpture, the glass gives me ideas in abundance. Ideas also come to me during intensive stages of work. The field of energy among the members of a glassmaking team is tangible, and that, if anything, inspires us to great achievements."

Sarpaneva speaks of the methods which he has developed. One of the most important ones is the "stick-air" or steam-blowing technique, used in his famous glass sculptures *Kayak* and *Orchid*. In 1954 *House Beautiful Magazine* from the United States elected *Orchid* as "the world's most beautiful object". Both works were awarded the Grand Prix at the Milan Triennial of 1954. They are clear glass, but around the same time the same method was also used in the I collection of glass, which in 1957 received the Grand Prix in Milan. The collection included a number of fine works of sculpture and large ellipsoid, square and triangular dishes and bowls. He developed a new series of "I colours" for these works. Timo Sarpaneva designs beautiful, aesthetic objects for use, always with some new idea. The concept of the I collection was an intermediary form between art and utility glass – elegant, light and limpid objects. Sarpaneva also designed a new i logo for the collection, which soon became the symbol of the Iittala glassworks. The colours of the i glassware immediately became standard features.

Other techniques developed by Sarpaneva are *Liekkiraita* (Flame stripe) and *Puumuottilasi* (Wooden mould glass) from 1963, *Archipelago* (1978) and *Claritas* (1983). The wooden mould technique had a profound influence on glassmaking in Finland. Sarpaneva used it in the 1960s to make his large pieces called *Finlandia*, which were blown and cast in wooden moulds. The mould burns, giving the piece a living surface. The same technique was used for collections of household glass and in making *Pack Ice* (4,5 x 9 m), the world's largest work of glass sculpture, for Expo 67 in Montreal, Canada. Sarpaneva designed the Finland pavilion at the world's fair.

Timo Sarpaneva has not restricted himself to glass, but has designed for many sectors of industry, including such specialist fields as book design, commercial art, and exhibition architecture. His designs of utility objects include work in cast iron for the Rosenlew corporation, steel for OPA, and in porcelain and pottery for Rosenthal AG. Sarpaneva has also designed textiles for the Pori Puuvilla and Tampella mills, and colour charts for the Winter paint factory. For Mäntyniemi, the new residence of the President of Finland, Sarpaneva designed a hand-made silver service (made by Kultakeskus) and *Marcel* collection of glassware, also made by hand at Iittala.

As artistic director of the Porin Puuvilla cotton mills from 1955 to 1965, Timo Sarpaneva designed the Karelia fabrics, the first export collection of the Finnish cotton industry. In 1965 he developed the important *Ambiente* paper-dyeing method for the Pori paper mills of the Rosenlew corporation. This technique provided new technical opportunities for colouring paper, and it received the Eurostar award in Vienna in 1965. The Eurostar is the highest distinction in this field. Sarpaneva also applied this technique in textiles, obtaining international patents for his inventions. *Ambiente* was used for making millions of metres of paper and interior fabrics.

Sarpaneva presented mysterious works of glass sculpture createad with the newest techniques at an exhibition held at the Opera House in Helsinki. This exhibition was one of the main events of Finland's period in the chairmanship of the EU in 1999 and of the Helsinki 2000 cultural capital programme.

Studio Pino Singoretto, Murano, Venice. Pino Singoretto with his assistants and Timo Sarpaneva.

Timo Sarpanevan arkisto

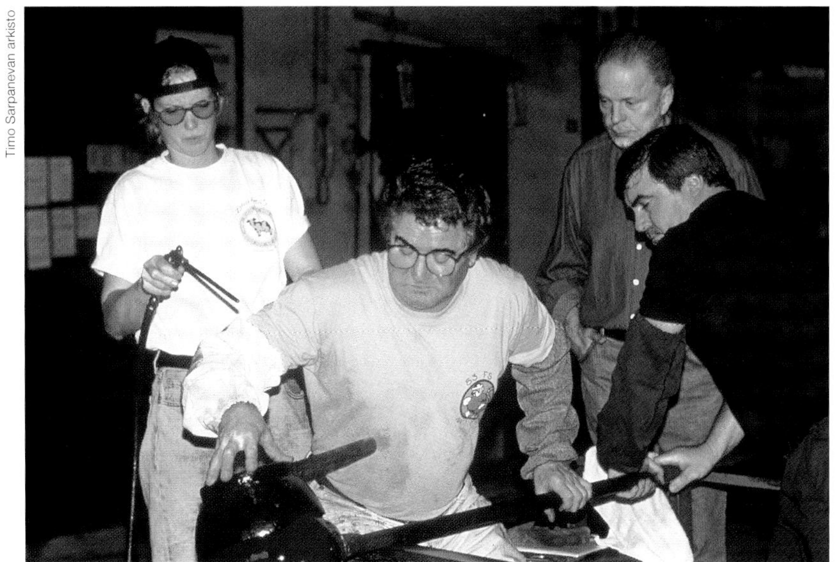

Timo Sarpaneva, Cormaris I – Heart of the Sea, *1999, length 28 cm, Studio Pino Signoretto, Murano, Venice. Timo Sarpaneva's archives.*

Markku Luhtala

▶▶*Timo Sarpaneva,* Liber Mundi – Books of the World, *1999, height 45, width 40 cm, Studio Pino Signoretto, Murano, Venice. Timo Sarpaneva's archives.*

"Dearest and most inspiring material for me is glass. It is magical, mystical and optically brilliant. It gives you the opportunity to make magnificent works. I have always had great craftsmen to help me when I have developed my methods. All the energy of the entire group is needed. But the artist must himself be excited about the project in order to be able to inspire his colleagues. It is from this that the synthesis leading to the end result originates. There is never any routine in this work, it is always new and creative."

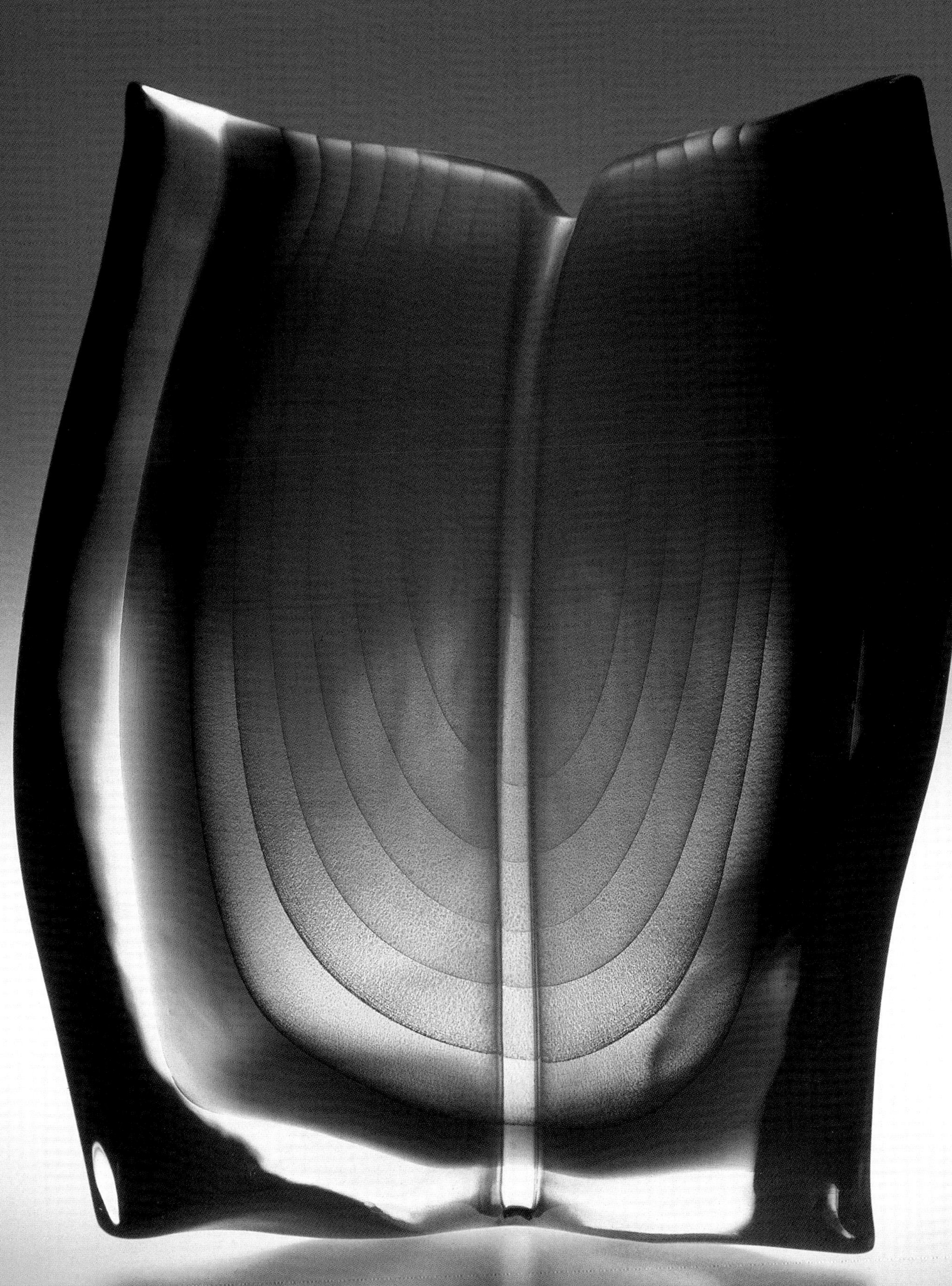

Kaj Franck
1911–1989

A Morning in Athens, Kaj Franck's wind chime of thin glass tubes with ball-shaped bubbles. When the wind strikes the tubes they chime and tinkle like little bells. Sound was the inspiration for the wind chime in 1954. It is told that Franck had been in Athens and had heard the carillons of the Greek Orthodox churches with the small and large bells ringing together in a joyous tune.

Kaj Franck's suspended wind chimes are made of individual blown glass tubes over 50 cm long. They were sold individually and the buyer could freely make his or her own chime of one or several tubes. Space and light permiting exhibitions have featured chimes of up to 100 tubes. The production of *A Morning in Athens* was resumed in the early 1990s for domestic and international exhibitions presenting Kaj Franck's life's work, for example at the Museum of Modern Art in New York.

The "immaterial" clear glass tubes of *A Morning in Athens* contain ball shapes typical of Franck. He preferred timeless basic shapes even in his experimental works, but would also give full rein to his gifts as an artist using colour. Working with the glassblowers, he developed new glassblowing techniques and revived, for example, filigree glass, the old forte of the Nuutajärvi glassworks. Kaj Franck's filigree work is modern painting with its lyrical, dramatic or joyous stripes and harmonies of colour. This was the method with which he made, for example, tropical fish of glass, cups and bottles. Spun glass is also an interesting technique, making the bowl look like a frozen hornet's nest. The exploded veil makes bowls, cups or fish figures of glass look like Tachist spot painting. The cups often include subtle combinations of different techniques, or cheerful pop colours. The most impressive symphonies of colour stripes are in Franck's *Ring* plates. These include pieces and collections of art glass. They have made their way into Finnish homes, museums and the antiques market.

Kaj Franck was artistic director and designer with the Nuutajärvi glassworks from 1950 to 1976. When he began to design the glassworks' new line of design his objective was to create functional, aesthetic and timeless glass for everyday use. He also began to make modern coloured utility glass, and the products became so popular that other glassworks took them as their example. There was also consistent effort in developing pressed glass, first coloured and then clear. Franck himself has designed hundreds of collections and series of glassware and unique pieces.

The Nuutajärvi glassworks has resumed the manufacture of Franck's coloured pressed glass of the 1950s and blown pourers, for example the *Kartio* (Cone) collection. These objects are among the figureheads of Finnish Functionalist design. Franck stressed that a good utility article should serve and be of a universal nature. For example, the pourers of the *Kartio* series are meant for both storing and serving beverages. Franck designed a great many pourers and carafes, of which one of the most exciting was *Kremlin kellot* (Bells of the Kremlin), a collection of coloured juice carafes from the 1950s. These ball-stoppered "onion-domed churches" are constructed of geometric spheres and cylinders. The carafes are in two parts permitting them to hold two kinds of fluids.

Kaj Franck has had a great influence on the everyday home environment of Finns. In addition to his years at Nuutajärvi he was also director of the product design department of the Arabia porcelain and ceramic works in Helsinki, as well as designing for Arabia. His most famous tableware collections are *Kilta* (1953) and *Teema* (1981). Franck also designed enamel and plastic vessels and containers and Finland's first modern stainless steel cutlery, the *Scandia* collection from 1952. The designed environment has also been influenced by Franck's many years as a teacher and instructor at the Institute of Arts and Crafts, the present-day University of Art and Design Helsinki. He was artistic director of the Institute.

Kaj Franck received numerous awards and prizes in recognition of his art in glass and his trailblazing achievements in industrial design, for example the Compasso d'Oro of Italy, the Prince Eugen Medal of Sweden and an honorary doctorate of the Royal College of Arts in London.

One of Kaj Franck's last works was a Japanese-style garden of Finnish stone, wood and plants in the courtyard of the Ministry of Education in Helsinki. Franck was also an avid gardener. Wherever he lived, in Helsinki or Nuutajärvi he would always create a garden as a work of art for his home.

▶ *Kaj Franck,* A Morning in Athens, *1954, mobile. Blown, clear glass tubes. Length c. 60 cm. Nuutajärven Lasi. Nuutajärvi. In production 1954–1975.*

Finnish Glass Museum/Timo Syrjänen

Helena Tynell, Forest, *glass sculpture. Cast, crushed colouring. Sizes 120 x 190 mm, 190 x 190 mm, 260 x 240 mm. Riihimäen Lasi, Riihimäki. In production until 1976.*

Helena Tynell
1918–

Visual compositions engraved in clear crystal: birds on the branch of the tree of life, flowers, leaves, circus acts, and the skyscrapers of Manhattan. The light plays with the thick glass, creating the illusion of floating images. Helena Tynell calls her engraved glass the graphics of light and lines. This was her speciality at the Riihimäki Glassworks from 1946 to 1957. She collaborated with the master engraver Teodor Käppi, who transferred the motifs and themes to crystal vases and bowls. Käppi also executed the bird and human figures for the jewellery in crystal and silver, which Helena Tynell put on show in 1950 at Finland House in New York. But this was also the decade when engraved luxury objects came to be regarded as outmoded, and the tradition of glass engraving was broken when Teodor Käppi retired.

Glass sculpture emerged as a new special area for Tynell. Her first glass sculptures, *Rialto* and *Castello*, were inspired by a trip to Italy in 1960. The angular structure of these abstract works of thick cast glass is underlined by marked cutting. The constructivist pieces were matched by free-form works and colour overlay often enhanced their expressiveness. One of Tynell's best-known sculptures is *Metsä* (Forest). It could also be described as a transparent castle wall, with blue and green "ivy" growing on it. The first exhibition of glass sculpture by Helena Tynell was held in an art gallery in Helsinki in 1966, followed by the first foreign showing in Chicago the next year. In the 1960s, Tynell also began her parallel career as a lamp designer for a German manufacturer. She has created her most recent works of glass sculpture in Germany.

For three decades Tynell designed not only art objects but also household glass for the Riihimäki Glassworks. The best-known of the latter designs are the colourful *Sun* bottles and *Pala* (Piece) vases from the 1960s. In 1963, Tynell received an award from the American Institute of Designers in recognition of her work in glass.

Helena Tynell has designed lamps and light fittings for the Bega Gantenbrick Leuchten factory of Germany for three decades. She began her work with the Bega lamps in 1961 and two years later her achievements were awarded the Gute Industriform prize. Lamps were not a new area for Helena Tynell. She was closely associated with the Finnish Taito lamp and light-fitting factory (1918–53). Her husband, Paavo Tynell, was the director of the works and the designer of the lamps. Paavo Tynell cooperated with Finland's leading architects, including Alvar Aalto.

Saara Hopea-Untacht
1925–1984

Saara Hopea's coloured, stackable tumblers are one of the symbols of modern Finnish design. They received the Silver Medal at the Milan Triennials of 1954, as an innovation of the period. Sara Hopea worked with Kaj Franck as a designer at the Nuutajärvi glassworks from 1952 to 1959.

Saara Hopea designed both coloured and clear glass, sets of glasses and individual vessels. Her elegant, clear *Flamingo* glasses, with a sphere on the slender stem, were awarded the Silver Prize at the Milan Triennials of 1957. A similar esprit is expressed by her limpid coloured ice-cream bowls, which were among the interesting innovations of the decade. Made of thick glass and with a touch of opulence Hopea's ruby-red *Bistro* stemmed glasses are tableware that one would still like to use today, but her works can now only be found n the antiques market.

In Saara Hopea's art glass simple and a patterned

Museum of Art and Design/Rauno Träskelin

▶ *Saara Hopea, Stackable tumblers, 1953. Blown, several colours. Height 8,5 cm. Nuutajärven Lasi, Nuutajärvi. In production until 1968.*

trends run parallel. The latter is particularly evident in crystal objects. Hopea carried on the traditional crystal line of the Nuutajärvi glassworks, with designs of minimalized vases, bowls and other products. The works include beautiful leaf-cut vases and bowls and platters decorated with right or bevelled angle designs.

During her last years at Nuutajärvi, Saara Hopea also designed jewellery for her family's company, the Ossian Hopea jeweller's of Porvoo. Jewellery now replaced glass as she took over the jewellery firm after the death of her father. Saara Hopea is one of the classic names of glass and jewellery design in Finland.

Nanny Still
1926 –

Glass sculpture about the linguistic kinship of Finnish and Hungarian! Nanny Still, a Finnish glass designer residing in Brussels, is known for applying bold concepts. On this occasion her Hungarian acquaintances had provoked her interest in the affinity of the Finnish and Hungarian languages, resulting in a series of glass sculptures. These works, with their magnificent colours, were created under the direction of the artist in glass studios in Belgium, Holland, France, Switzerland and Germany. The fascinating collection was presented to the Hungarian public at an exhibition of Nanny Still's works at the Museum of Applied Arts in Budapest and the Szolnok gallery in 1998–99.

The sculptures take as their starting point the many words that have remained similar in Finnish and Hungarian for thousands of years. *Vesi-Viz* (Water) is interpreted as dynamic waves with the shine of water, while *Metsä-Messze* (Forest) is a cubist composition of dark violet and transparently blue-veiled glass. The latter can be seen, for example, as an interpretation of the light and shade of the deep forest. *Kuu-Hold* (Moon) resembles the traditional Finnish round loaf of rye bread with a hole in the centre. It is a bluish gold 'cratered' disc with a hole in the middle, and based on the Chinese symbol *bi*, expressing the sky, earth, fire and water. According to Nanny Still, her own nostalgic memories of Finnish rye bread may also have inspired the piece.

Finnish Glass Museum/Paul Louis

Nanny Still, Forest, Messze Woods, *1993, glass sculpture. Pâte de verre technique. Height 35,5 cm, length 28,5 cm. Glasgestaltung, Brachelen, Germany.*

The Finnish public knows Nanny Still as a designer of the Riihimäki Glassworks. From 1949 to 1976, she designed a wide range of household glassware and art glass. Her best-known collections are *Harlekiini* (Harlequin) and *Flindari*. Dating from 1959 the Harlequins with their Mediterranean turquoise hues and geometric shapes have been standard favourites in Finland, and in the United States the *Flindari* series with its surface in relief earned Nanny Still the International Design Award of 1965. Many other sets of glassware by Still have exciting features, for example the jade, pink and green *Tzarinas*, inspired by the era of the tsars, or the Turkish-influenced *Sultans*.

Although Still moved to Brussels in 1959, she has not turned her back on her Finnish work. She went on to forge a Continental European career as a designer of glass, porcelain and lamps. She had a dream commission in the 1960s for the design of all light fittings and glassware of the Hilton hotels of Brussels and London.

Finnish Glass Museum/Timo Syrjänen

◀ *Nanny Still,* Harlequin, *1958, glassware. Blown turquoise and clear glass. Height c. 10–28 cm. Riihimäen Lasi, Riihimäki. In production 1959–71.*

iittala/Timo Kauppila

Oiva Toikka, the Trojan War, *1987, installation. Free blown and cast. 100 x 175 x 30 cm, 140 kg. Nuutajärven Lasi, Nuutajärvi.*

Oiva Toikka
1931–

Glass and opera at the Finnish National Opera in the spring of 1999. Oiva Toikka designed the costumes and sets for "Orlando Paladino", Joseph Haydn's colourful opera on the theme of chivalry. This was the fourth time he cooperated with the director Lisbeth Landefort. The stage was like blue and white porcelain, with modern, graphic structural and natural motifs. The avant-garde rococo milieu represents the Hungarian palace of Prince Esterhazy. Haydn composed the opera in 1782 for Prince Esterhazy's own stage.

Glass by Oiva Toikka could easily be compared with the opera, for there was also an exhibition of Toikka's works in the foyer. Blue and white graphic design appears, for example, in *Eilisen totuus* (Yesterday's truth). The headgear of fantasy figures in glass were no doubt an inspiration for the fountain-hat of the wonderful Amore ballerina figure, the seated lion helmet of Orlando, and the helmets with Greek temples worn by the male dancers. The yellow costume of Angelica in the opera alludes to the yellow Angelica in glass, and the fluffy dresses of the ballerinas, dressed as sheep, are like the white glass thread of Toikka's piece *Sateet tulivat* (And the rains came).

The viewer is fascinated by the colourful fantasy creatures staring out of the transparent glass cubes. With the cubes laid in several rows, one feels like one is looking at a Jacques Cousteau documentary about jellyfish and other wonders of the deep seas. Toikka can make anything he desires out of his cubes, including 'skyscrapers' which he presented in New York (1989). He is also familiar with monuments, and the exhibition included glass versions of Stonehenge and the *Trojan War*. In the opera Orlando there is a battle between knights and barbarians, while in Toikka's *Trojan War* stark white figures stand stoically as an expression of peace, or at least a truce.

There was also pop art. Toikka's breakthrough exhibition in Helsinki in 1966 featured his high diamond-engraved *Bambu* (Bamboo) vases, which were also on show a year later in Stockholm in an exhibition held jointly with Bertil Vallien of Sweden. Toikka's *Lollipop* sculptures, multicoloured *Pampula* vases, and clear-glass *Cucumber Jar* pieces were on show in 1969 in London. The Victoria & Albert Museum purchased *Lollipop* Isle and *Cucumber* Jar. In the following year this new star of Finnish glass design was awarded the Nordic Lunning prize.

A glass sculptor of imaginative scope, Toikka has also designed many successful series of household glassware for the Nuutajärvi Glassworks. The *Pioni* (Peony) tableware collection, dating back to the 1970s, is still a staunch favourite. No less popular are Toikka's glass birds, which are manufactured as a series of art glass objects. There are now almost a hundred species of birds, some of which were on show in the restaurant of the Opera foyer.

During the 1990s Oiva Toikka has been a professor at the Department of Glass and Ceramic Design at the University of Art and Design in Stockholm, inspiring Finnish and Swedish design students to participate in joint glassmaking events.

Glass and Opera! Oiva Toikka's art in glass is like an operatic production of transparent palaces, monuments and dramatic fantasy figures.

◀◀ *Oiva Toikka* Sateet tulivat *(And the rains came), 1995, glass sculpture. Cast. 90 x 120 x 100 cm. Nuutajärven Lasi, Nuutajärvi. Photo: Iittala/Timo Kauppila.*

Heikki Orvola
1943–

The Aperto Vetro glass biennial of Venice in late 1989 and early 1999. Heikki Orvola's *Grand Canal*, a group of glass columns almost a metre high greets the flow of people in the Renaissance passageway of the Palace of the Doges. Grand Canal is Heikki Orvola's homage to Venice. Ornate columns in a shallow basin, the "canal", suggest the posts to which the gondolas are moored. The gondola posts often have a spiral stripe pattern. The piece also bears the meaning of the four seasons.

Heikki Orvola is attracted to Cubism and Russian avant-garde art of the early 1900s. His Cubist *Maya* figures in glass, reclining on their sides, allude to Francisco Goya's famous oil painting *The Nude Maya*. Orvola's *Mayas* were made as part of the Pro Arte collection (1999) of the Nuutajärvi Glassworks. His most recent works in glass include a beautiful bowl in the art déco spirit, commissioned by the shop of the Bagatti Valsecchi Museum of Italy. The design on the bowl replicates the pattern on the floor of one of the rooms in the museum.

In *Grand Canal* and the *Bagatti Valsecchi* bowl, Orvola used sand blasting technique to engrave the patterns. Ornament and delicate foliate motifs in this technique were already on show in 1983 at Orvola's breakthrough exhibition in Helsinki. The motifs were made on shiny lustre glass. This exhibition was a rehabilitation of ornamental art, for it included a number of magnificent miniature textiles embroidered by hand. After presenting his collection also in Amsterdam, Orvola left Nuutajärvi to become a freelance artist. He received a grant and spent the following three years working uniquely on embroidered miniature textiles. This was followed by a collection of printed fabrics for Marimekko, and in 1987 Orvola, originally trained as a ceramist, was invited to design ceramics for the Arabia factory, and to apply his ornamental skills to luxury tableware and items.

In the 1990s Heikki Orvola has mainly designed unique art objects for the Nuutajärvi Glassworks. He was in the permanent employ of Nuutajärvi from 1968 to 1983, creating among other works some ten streamlined sets of glassware. *Aurora*, a set of glassware from his early years, is still being manufactured. Orvola's most recent utility object is the conical *Evergreen* vase, made in various colours. He prefers to work in timeless, streamlined forms, as is also shown by the tableware designed by him for Arabia.

Iittala/Timo Kauppila

Heikki Orvola, Maya, *1995, glass sculptur. Blown and cast. Nuutajärven Lasi, Nuutajärvi.*

Iittala/Timo Kauppila

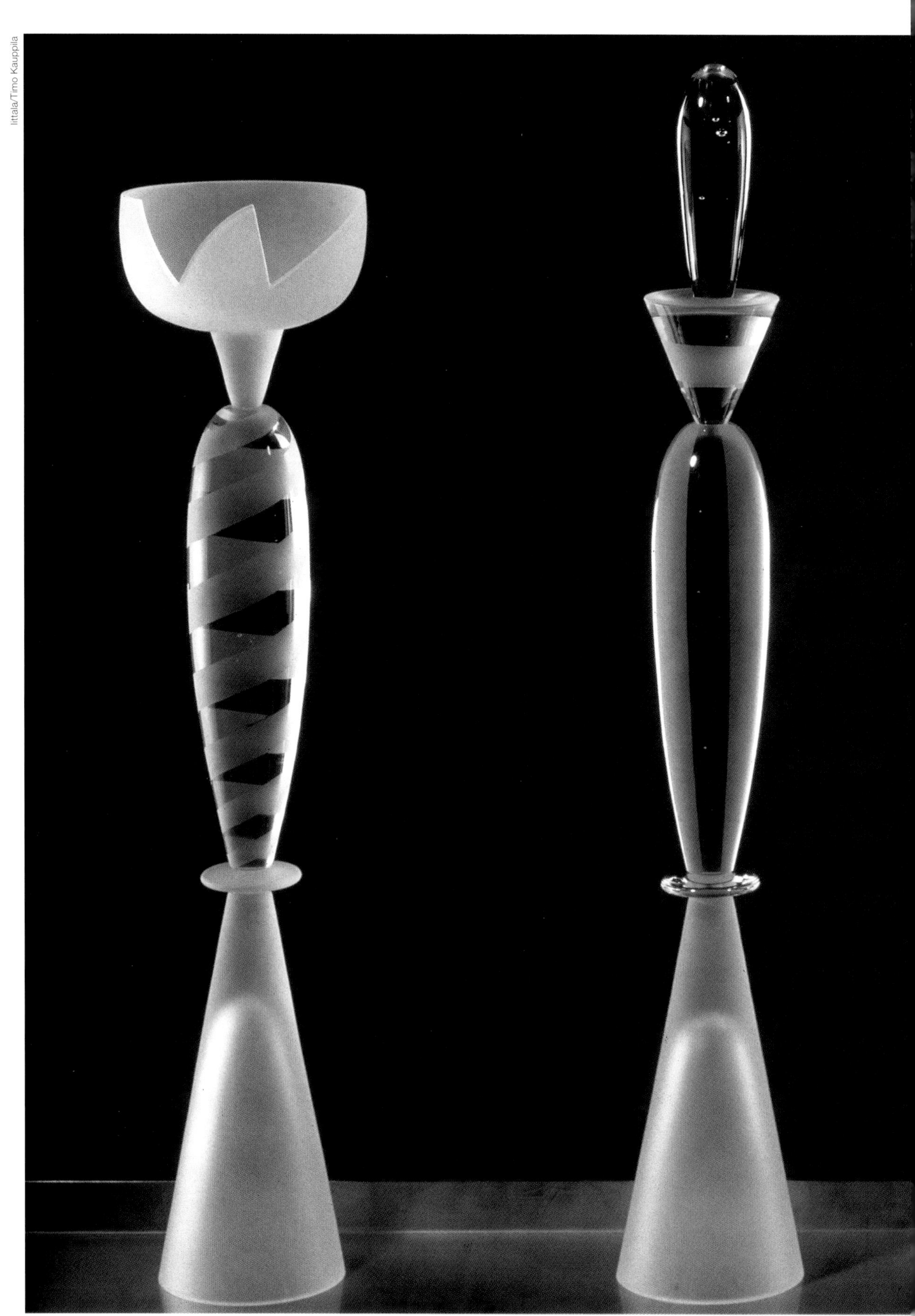

Heikki Orvola, Grand Canal, *Venice, Aperto Vetro, 1998, a four-part installation. Free blown and cast. 94 x 150 x 35 cm. Nuutajärven Lasi, Nuutajärvi.*

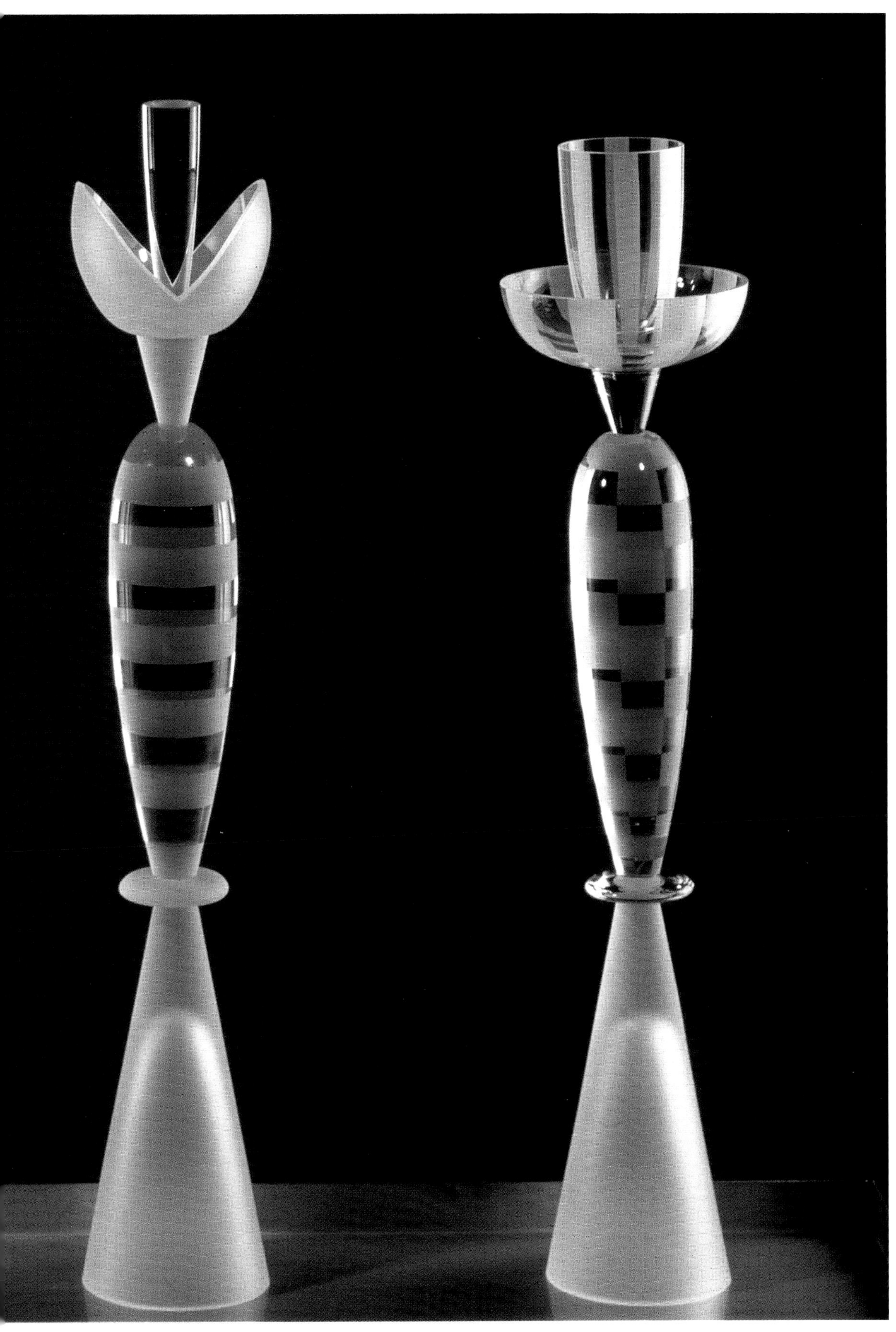

Kerttu Nurminen
1943–

Kerttu Nurminen's new Palazzo collection of filigree glass is an exciting combination of princely luxury items and contemporary art. The red-orange goblets in particular, with their net designs, and the "whirlpool" dish play with the eye like works of kinetic art. Kerttu Nurminen's visits to Venice with its palazzi, the home of filigree glass, have clearly inspired her. In 1998 she held a solo exhibition in Venice, and her works were also on show at the Aperto Vetro biennial of glass design.

The theme of water appears in different forms in Nurminen's works, for example in the works on show in Venice. It is expressed in the patterns and designs of the vases and dishes as whirlpools, autumn leaves on the surface of a pond, a flurry of snow, rain or as a swimmer motif. The water theme was an easy choice with Venice in mind. "In Venice one is surrounded by water, and so it is in Finland, too. That is where the ideas came from," says Kerttu Nurminen. Air and water also inspired Nurminen's *Mondo* collection of glassware (1988), her great professional success. Soon after being introduced, *Mondo* was purchased by the Museum of Modern Art in New York for its sales collection.

Kerttu Nurminen lives in the glassmaking village of Nuutajärvi. With its old manor and glassworks, Nuutajärvi is a charming idyll in a rural setting. In her unique works, Nurminen has depicted the nature of Nuutajärvi to such a degree and so beautifully that she deserves to be called the landscape artist of glass. These works include highly painterly "glass watercolour" vases, with subjects such as a pond with water lilies, tadpoles learning to swim, and writhing blindworms.

"The outdoors and the natural surroundings of Nuutajärvi influence my work. The seasons mean a great deal to me. In spring and summer I choose light colours, but in autumn and winter light tones or loud colours do not seem to suit the environment. There are many colours in nature in the various seasons. People say that autumn is dreary and grey, but there are many colours even in rainy weather. And even the air is coloured. Some mornings are violet while others are greenish grey. Rowing on the lake in summer, I see the water, sky and forest like striped layers of colour in the landscape. This impression is best seen when swimming on one's back in the lake."

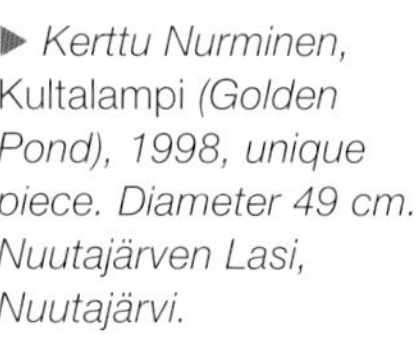

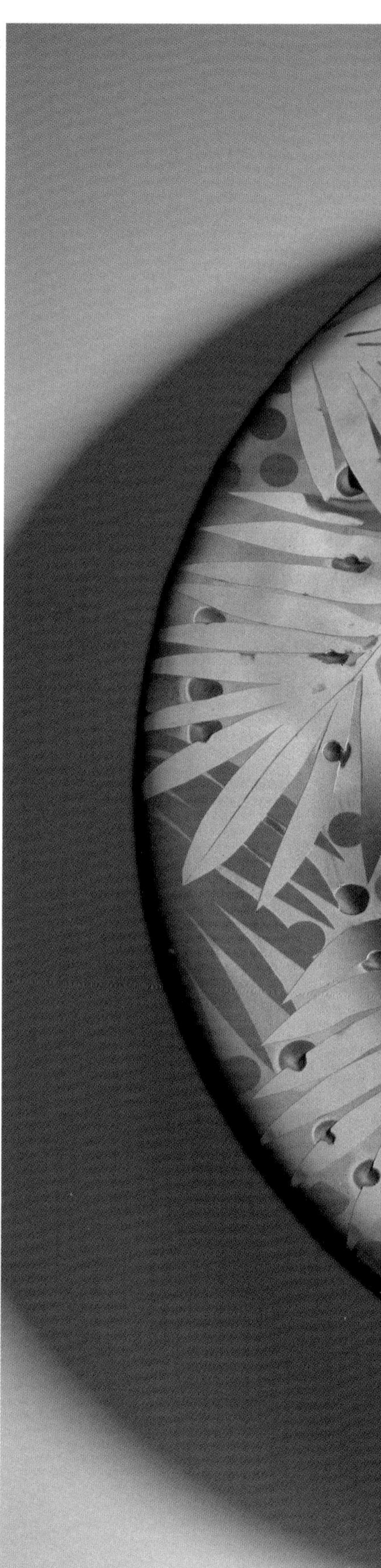

Iittala/Timo Kauppila

▶ *Kerttu Nurminen,* Kultalampi *(Golden Pond), 1998, unique piece. Diameter 49 cm. Nuutajärven Lasi, Nuutajärvi.*

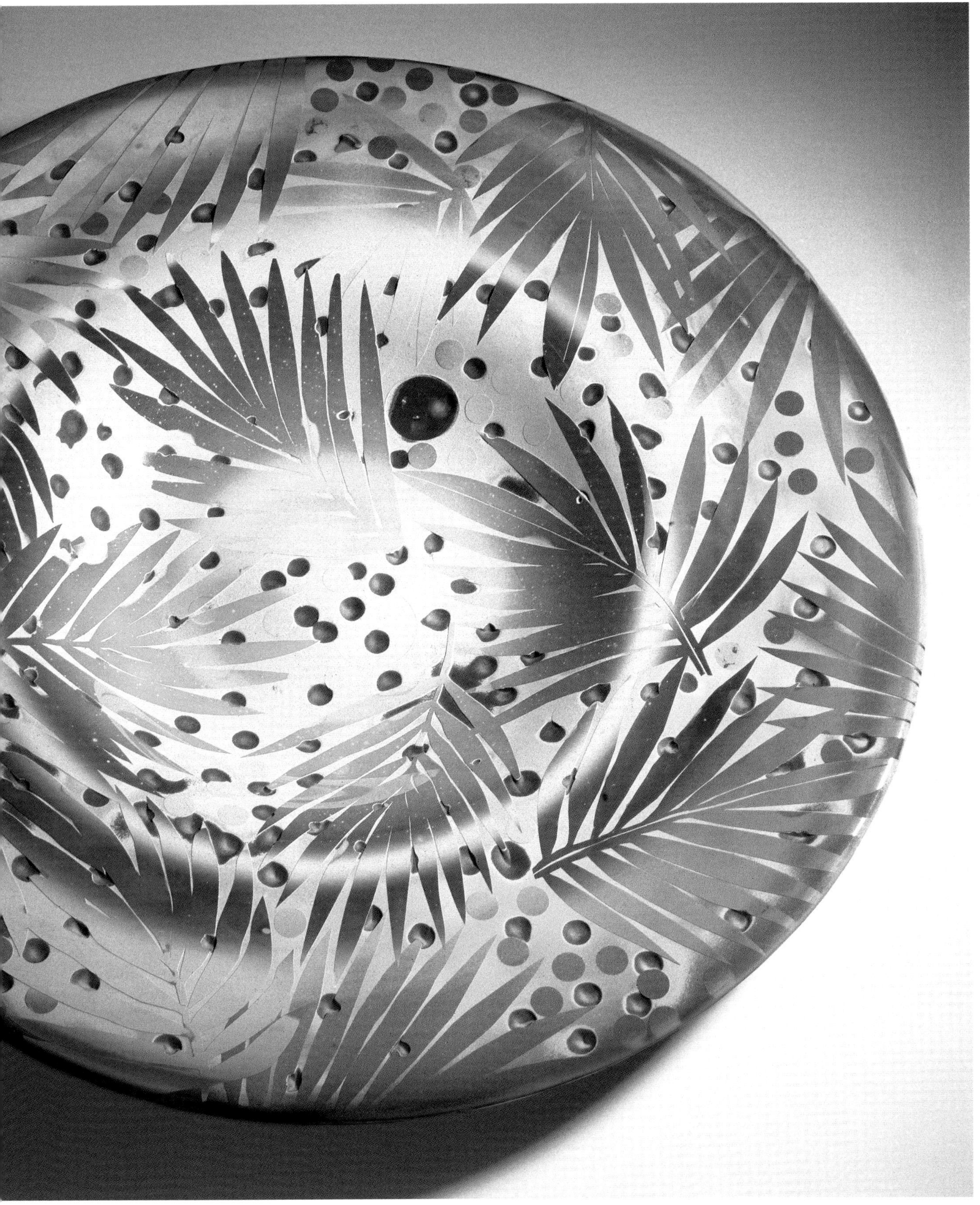

Iittala/Timo Kauppila

Markku Salo, Helle (Kuumuus, Heat), 1998, unique piece. Pâte de verre technique. Diameter 51 cm. Private studio, Nuutajärvi.

Markku Salo
1954–

The caves of the Retretti Art Centre in Punkaharju, in Eastern Finland, in the summer of 1998. The great favourite of visitors is an industrial robot performing a choreographed ballet with luxury pots designed by Markku Salo. The robot reaches out with its long arm, taking one pot at a time from a shelf for its dance, returning all the pots to their right places. There is a more restrained performance in the cave known as "The Chapel", where an undulating mosaic cover entitled *The Birth of the Dream* brings forth kinetic impressions. This work is made of soot and clear crushed glass spread over sand. Hung above one of the ponds is *Winter in Venice*, a large, ice-white web of glass. This work was exhibited that same autumn at the Aperto Vetro biennial in Venice as a partition in a Venetian palazzo.

Originally educated as an industrial designer, Markku Salo changed jobs from Salora television sets to an involvement with the Nuutajärvi glassworks in 1983. A few years were spent solely with mass-produced items. One of Salo's first art objects was *Hallanvaara* (Imminent Frost) a giant bird of glass and steel with wings moved by an electric motor. *Huvimaja* (Gazebo), a teepee-like Lapp hut of transparent glass, is also a large piece. Upon entering it, the visitor feels like he or she is floating among the graphic motifs on the walls.

"Where do my ideas come from? The initial spark may be an image in my mind, but when I am making the piece I think with my hands, while the glassblowers assist me. I make most of the moulds and metal parts myself, and I carry out the finishing work. Assembling the pieces is mostly my work, too."

Markku Salo's lyrical side is best expressed in his smaller art objects, in which he has often used the amphora shape, combining it with his own ideas. These works include net-blown and markedly stylized amphora shape, in hues such as desert sand or bright pop colours. He also makes refined luxury items, such as the amphora *Moderate Pollen*. This beautiful object was blown from yellow glass and the designs were marked by sand blasting. "It was one of my first ornamental objects. I got the idea from the weather forecast on the radio, where the words 'moderate pollen' were repeated. The natural forms of my mental images fly around in the amphora."

Markku Salo has introduced exciting, large spatial works into Finnish glass art. These works enter into a "dialogue" with the viewers.

Tapio Wirkkala, Tapio *glassware, 1952, Iittala.*

Iittala

Kaj Franck, série Kartio*, 1956, Nuutajärven Lasi.*

Iittala/Markku Luhtala

▼ *Kerttu Nurminen,* Mondo *glassware, 1988. Nuutajärven Lasi.*

Iittala

Iittala/Antti Kylänpää

Heikki Orvola, Aurora *glassware, 1972. Nuutajärven Lasi.*

Iittala/Markku Luhtala

Timo Sarpaneva, Marcel *glassware, 1993. Iittala.*

The Story of Arabia

Hannele Nyman

An advertisement from 1929 for the Arabia porcelain factory states: "The honour of your home calls for a new Arabia dinner service." This was not far from the truth. During its 125 years of existence Arabia has become a concept in its own right in Finland. For many it is synonymous with china and porcelain. Almost all Finns have some personal connection with the products of Arabia – through the objects of one's grandparents, parents or one's own home. The Arabia porcelain factory has also been instrumental in creating the concept of Finnish Design.

Arabia is a versatile plant, which has produced not only household tableware but also bricks, tiles, tiled stoves, sanitary porcelain, electrotechnical porcelain and ornamental objects. Since 1932, it has had an art department that has earned the factory world renown. Although the decades of the Arabia factory include many historical changes, expansion, restructuring and changes in ownership and design, the core elements of Arabia have survived.

The life of the Arabia factory is a fascinating combination of past, present and future. There is a functioning unity of the factory, its workers and designers, creators of things new, and its memory, the factory museum founded in 1948. An arena and window for all who are interested in Arabia and ceramics is the museum's gallery, with its rich and versatile presentation of contemporary ceramics and the history and products of Arabia.

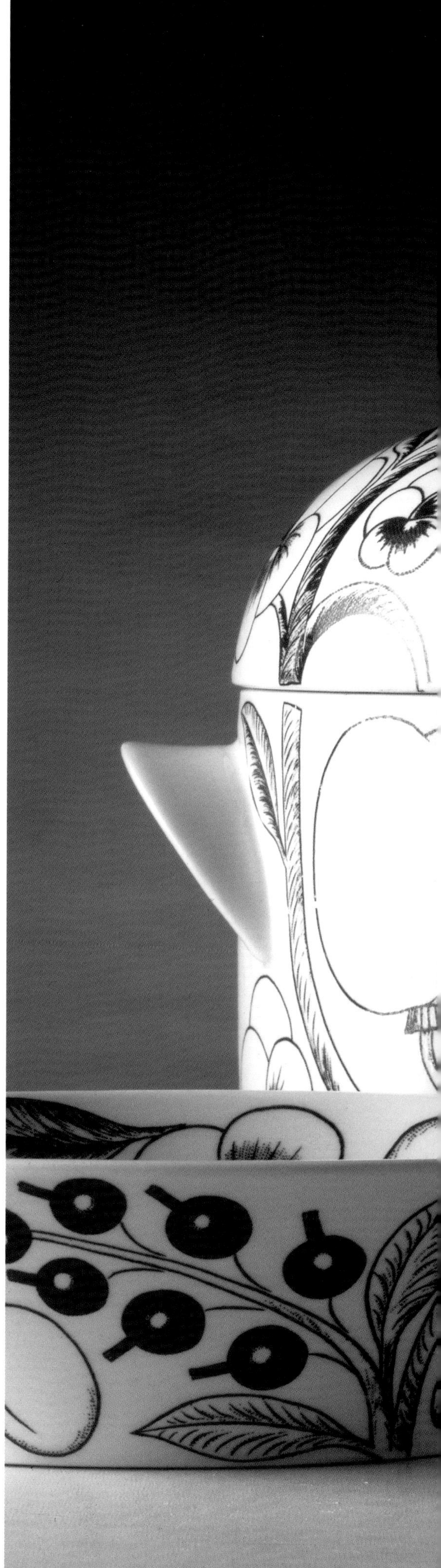

▶ *Birger Kaipiainen,* Paratiisi *(Paradise)* *dinner service, 1970-74, 1994–, Arabia*

Design Forum Finland/Rauno Träskelin

Arabia Museum/Timo Kauppila

First issue products 19–22 October 1874, Arabia.

Arabia Museum

Asian Pheasants*, tureen, 1876-1950, Arabia.*

Arabia Museum/Timo Kauppila

The Toivo dinner service 1912–17, Arabia

Arabia Museum/Gero Mülius

Thure Öberg, Hand-painted Finnish landscapes 1900/1925 Arabia

In November 1873 the Senate of Finland gave the Rörstrand porcelain factory official permission to establish a subsidiary plant in Helsinki. The first products came out of the ovens in October 1874. This marked the beginning of the long history of Arabia's fascinating products. The name "Arabia" came from the location where the factory was established, in the outskirts of Helsinki at a place known as the meadows of the "Land of Canaan" and the "Arabia" villa lot. The original Arabia products were simple, undecorated tableware – plates, dishes, mugs, storage jars etc., sanitary porcelain and dinner services decorated with copper prints. A soup tureen decorated with copper prints requires the work of many skilled workers, many of whom were women. The ceramic paste was mixed in a mill and transported to the casting department, where lathe-turned plaster moulds were filled for the casting. After the initial raw firing, the ornamental pattern was transferred from a skillfully engraved copper plate with the aid of silk paper. The ornamental patterns and designs passed from one factory to another in Europe along with the plates and engravers. The ornamental firing and the glaze firing took place in the round kilns, into which the pieces were loaded by hand. After the kiln had slightly cooled, the firing capsules and their content were piled aside, the pieces were inspected and finished, taken to the warehouse, carefully packaged and shipped to clients.

From 1893 to 1916 the Arabia factory was headed by Gustav Herlitz, who was responsible for the rapid development of the works. New kilns and furnaces for the raw, glaze and enamel firing stages were built, as well as a tile workshop and a decoration department. Arabia participated in exhibitions ever since the 1870s, at first with showpieces by French porcelain painters originally from the Rörstrand factory. Herlitz began to employ art consultants, such as the architect Jac. Ahrenberg, and in 1896 the factory hired its first designer on a full-time basis, Thure Öberg. Öberg was particularly skilled in making sub-glaze decoration, and he was responsible for many dinner services and vases for representative use. Arabia's products were awarded a gold medal at the Paris World Fair in 1900 and exports grew to include the United States among other countries.

Arabia's Own Line 1910s–1930s

During the 1900s the factory's own line was reinforced and became prominent. A dinner service design contest was held in 1912. The winner was the versatile designer and artist Eric O. W. Ehrström. In 1916 Arabia passed into Finnish ownership with Carl Gustaf Herlitz, son of G. Herlitz, as its new director. Carl-Gustaf boldly undertook reforms of the plant in a large-scale project including electrification, a new mixing mill, round and ornament firing kilns, improved quality and a diversification of production.

An extensive programme of renewal continued throughout the 1920s. The buildings were renewed, a modern laboratory was opened, the plan bought its first lorry, Arabia bought the Turku Porcelain Factory, and there was cooperation with the Arnold group of Germany from 1923 until 1927, when Arabia purchased the Lidköping Porcelain Factory in Sweden, and acquired a majority holding in the Rörstrand company. In 1929 the factory built the world's longest tunnel kiln (112 metres). The adoption of the once-firing method for making sanitary porcelain made it possible to use this technique on 60% of all household ware, which spelt considerable economic benefits. At the turn of the 1920s and '30s more and more money was invested in advertising. There was talk of a "major advertising offensive". The Arabia plant employed new designers, including Thyra Lundgren, Friedl Holzer-Kjellberg and Greta Lisa Jäderholm-Snellman, who were given the task of renewing the factory's range of products.

In 1932, Kurt Ekholm was appointed artistic director of Arabia and the factory's legendary art department evolved around him. New designers included Toini Muona, Aune Siimes, Michael Schilkin and Birger Kaipiainen, followed by Rut Bryk, Kyllikki Salmenhaara and others in the 1940s. Arabia Art Department made its breakthrough at the Paris World Fair of 1937, and it reaped success at the Milan Triennials and its own exhibitions both in Finland and abroad.

One of the unique features of the Arabia Art Department was the complete freedom of action which it granted to its designers and artists in their creative work. Over the years, the artists introduced ideas and innovations for the benefit of industrial manufacture. The need for the art department was questioned from time to time. In the 1940s Ekholm had to defend it following criticism of its exhibition in Stockholm. One of the reviews suspected that the Arabia Art Department was only " a flower in the lapel" with no role in the design of utility objects. Ekholm responded and said that the policy followed by Arabia had proven its merits: "The achievements of our designers, which are enjoying artistic freedom and unanimously underscored by Scandinavian critics, are due solely to the fact that they have been allowed to concentrate undisturbed on their own works."

Abundance and Practical Beauty 1930s–1940s

In the 1930s, Arabia was Europe's largest porcelain factory. In 1928 it had 527 employees; six years later this figure had doubled. In 1937, the production pro-

Arabia Museum/Timo Kauppila

Greta-Lisa Jäderholm-Snellman, LB *coffee service 1933-46, Arabia.*

Arabia Museum/Timo Kauppila

Kurt Ekholm, Sinivalko *(Blue-White) 1936–54, Arabia.*

gramme encompassed some 30,000 individual products. Ekholm's *Sinivalko* (Blue-White) service is an example of a functionalist design of practical beauty, while Reinhard Richter's richly decorated *AS* dinner service expressed a warm, cosy and home-like mood. The factory remained in operation during the second world war. Most of Arabia's products were exported. The prevailing shortage of materials led to innovation, such as coloured paste. It was difficult to obtain pure materials and the paste for faience and porcelain began to be deliberately coloured. The yellowish ferra faience, for example, became popular.

In 1946 Ekholm was succeeded by Kaj Franck as artistic director. The design department operating under Franck hired Kaarina Aho, Ulla Procopé, Göran Bäck, Raija Uosikkinen and Ester Tomula. The art department carried on as a separate unit, and the applied arts department under Olga Osol was established to carry on the work of the department for "More beautiful everyday ware" and the hand-painting section. Friedl Holzer-Kjellberg's "rice porcelain" began to be made in 1942. In 1947 Arabia was included in the Wärtsilä group of companies and the Arabia Museum was opened on the top floor of the factory in 1948. Speaking at the opening of the museum, Kurt Ekholm noted: "The rooms here are higher than on the other floors, and the wide perspectives of the view agree with the concept of the museum."

An Everyday Aesthetic – 1950s

The 1950s were dominated by Kaj Franck's views and visions and the concept of Finnish Design. Franck's *Kilta* series of tableware was begun in the 1940s, and it came into production in 1953. *Kilta* was not a service in the traditional sense, but rather a system of tableware items. The underlying idea was to save both costs and storage space with a few basic items based on strict geometric forms that could serve various functions. *Kilta* was not immediately popular, but once established in the market, it gained immense popularity. Ulla Procopé's oven-proof *Liekki* (Flame) collection was taken into production in 1958.

At the Milan Triennials of 1951, 1954 and 1957, the designers and artists of Arabia received a considerable number of prizes. Finnish and Scandinavian design began to tour the word in exhibitions. A significant role in this process was played H. O. Gummerus, who became head of public relations at Arabia in 1949. The factory also hired new artists and designers, including Gunvor Olin-Grönqvist, Raija Tuumi, and Franceska and Richard Lindh. There were also many visiting foreign artists and designers at the Art Department during the 1950s and '60s.

The Arabia Art Department in the 1940s. From the left: Aune Siimes, Michael Schilkin, Toini Muona, Friedl Holzer-Kjellberg, Kurt Ekholm, Lea von Mickwitz, Birger Kaipiainen and Rut Bryk.

Toini Muona (1904–1987) was a recognized forerunner and predecessor who remained loyal to Arabia throughout her professionally creative years from 1931 until 1970. Various bowls, dishes and tall, narrow vases known as "straws" were typical of Muona's oeuvre.

Finnish Tableware 1960s–1970s

The Finnish Design phenomenon lived on in the 1960s. Finnish dining culture was promoted. Ulla Procopé's *Ruska* was made of a new material for dining services, oven-proof stoneware, which was given a rustic brown glaze. Procopé's *Valencia*, in turn, was richly painted with cobalt blue designs. Kaarina Aho's *Palapeli* (Jigsaw) service was based on the idea of total stackability, with the plates serving as the lids of the bowls. Göran Bäck specialized in services and kitchenware for large household units. Kaj Franck was in favour of anonymity in the design of household ware. Many of his contemporary designers at Arabia have partly remained "anonymous", although the products that they designed are known. New designers included Heljä Liukko-Sundström and Inkeri Leivo. Kaipiainen's 'bead birds' were prize-winners at Milan in 1960, and his *Sea of Violets* was widely noted at Expo '67 in Montreal. Although Kaipiainen concentrated on unique pieces in his oeuvre, his *Paradise* service aptly reflects the joyous side of the late 1960s and early 1970s.

The economic recession of the 1970s led to a Scandinavian "elephantine wedding" – the merger of Arabia and Rörstrand from 1975 until 1977. The factories divided the materials with Arabia concentrating on stoneware and Rörstrand working in porcelain and faience. The new joint production strategy resulted in major change at Arabia, where both the production programme and the factory's Art Department were radically downsized. These developments led to considerable debate in Finland, where the discontinuation of the *Kilta* and *Paradise* services as well as the rice porcelain were regarded as national scandals. Claims that the art department was unnecessary were not accepted.

The new stage of collaboration was regarded as the sell-out and loss of an important element of the Finnish identity. *Kilta*, *Paradise* and rice china were all given the status of national symbols. Their discontinuation was regarded as a sign of general defeatism in industry and a rejection of design. The Swedish press also suspected a bias in these matters, and it was felt that Arabia had sold its soul by reducing its art department.

The merger agreement was revoked after the trial period, since "mediocrity does not pay", as noted in a press release from Arabia. Reforms were needed, but the wrong means had been chosen this time. The press rejoiced over the separation of the companies: "We

Arabia Museum/Gero Mülius

Ulla Procopé, Valencia *dinner service 1960–, Arabia.*

Arabia

Inkeri Leivo, Arctica *dinner service 1979–, Arabia.*

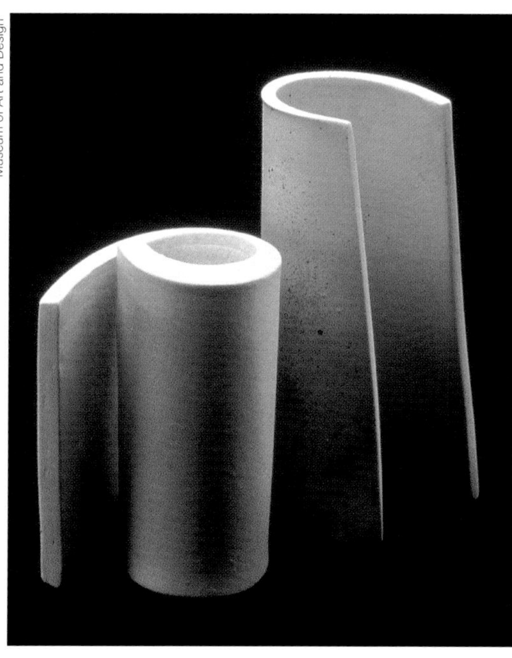

Museum of Art and Design

▶ Kyllikki Salmenhaara's (1915–1981) years at Arabia (1947–61) involved experiments with ceramic pastes and glazes. She liked to wheel-turn all her objects herself and she sought forms that emerged, unforced, according to the innate laws of the materials themselves. During the 1960s and '70s Salmenhaara taught at the University of Art and Design in Helsinki, where she had considerable influence on the training of Finnish ceramic designers.

feel that the products of Arabia are our own again", "Rejecting the Finnishness of Arabia was like selling the country at cut-rate prices", and "The reactions to the announced discontinuation of cooperation were so immediate, honest and joyful... Finnish design, and particularly porcelain, one of its figureheads, is important for national identity alone."

At the close of the 1970s came another major reform. The factory adopted new, modern tunnel kilns, and thin-walled stoneware was introduced – Gunvor Olin-Grönqvist's *Tea for Two* and Inkeri Leivo's *Arctica*. A new set of national dinner services had been created.

Arabia/Timo Kauppila

Pekka Paikkari, Toy *shaker 1997–, Arabia.*

Contemporary Design 1980s–1990s

The *Kilta* service made a come-back in the 1980s as the *Teema* service, and the manufacture of *Paradise* was also resumed. Kati Tuominen-Niittylä, Pekka Paikkari and Dorrit von Fieandt were new designers hired by Arabia. There were again visiting designers, such as Rudy Autio, Howard Smith, Kristina Riska, Jun Kaneko and Fujiwo Ishimoto. The Pro Arte collection was introduced in 1988, consisting of experimental design products in small series. The collections change every few years, and works from them are taken into large-scale production.

In 1990 the Hackman group acquired ownership of Arabia and Rörstrand, as well as Iittala and Nuutajärvi, Finland's leading glassworks. The trend is to create new design in all areas. The boldness and vision of the 1990s are represented, for example, by Kati Tuominen's *Roma* dish and *Storybirds* pourers, Pekka Paikkari's *Toy* shaker, or Heikki Orvola's *24h* service. During the 1990s, the coveted Design Plus award of the Ambiente Fair in Hamburg went to Arabia products on three occasions: in 1994 to *Storybirds*, in 1997 to *24h*, and in 1998 to Pia Törnell's *Tilda* collection.

Arabia engages in projects with outside designers, as for example in Stefan Linfdors's *EgO* coffee-cup collection in 1998. Each year, young ceramists train at the Art Department. In 1999, they included Matti Pyykkö, Nathalie Lahdenmäki and Tony Alffström, all of whom received honorary mentions in the Mino ceramic contest in 1998. The strength of Arabia's own designers lies in their familiarity with the requirements of the factory and its production processes and their opportunities to engage in long-term design work, Kati Tuominen-Niittylä and Pekka Paikkari have also enjoyed international success, both as designers and artists.

Arabia/Timo Kauppila

Kati Tuominen-Niittylä, Storybirds *pourers 1993–, Arabia.*

Arabia/Timo Kauppila

Heikki Orvola, 24 h *dinner service 1997–, Arabia.*

Arabia/Timo Kauppila

▲ Pekka Paikkari (born 1960) has long been fascinated by bottle shapes. At first, his own ceramic bottles were small, round pieces, but before long they started to have a slender neck. "You can express anything with bottles. Now, they have become more of an image of the bottle, a means of communication." Paikkari has worked at the Arabia Art Department since the mid-1980s.

▲ Characteristic features of Kristina Riska's (born 1960) works are fragility and an aesthetic austerity. The essence and character of a piece emerge as Kristina constructs layer by layer. Each work is a separate individual, a freely constructed piece. Kristina was a visiting designer with Arabia in the 1980s, and she still has a studio in the factory building.

F Rut Bryk (1916–1999) began her ceramic design career in 1942 with fairy tale-like visual motifs. In the 1950s she developed a technique in which plaques with designs in raised lines were coloured with an intensively hued translucent glaze. From the turn of 1960s Bryk concentrated on plaque composition of an increasingly abstract and monumental nature. Jäävirta (River of Ice) made in 1990 for the new residence of the President of Finland as Bryk's last design at Arabia.

◀ The Seenas, Terhi Juurinen (born 1945) and Riitta Siira (born 1948), studied ceramic design and pottery at the University of Art and Design. At the time, Kyllikki Salmenhaara was encouraging her students to make works in small series. The Seenas' production concept was simple and distinct: to make utility objects based on the considerations of unaffectedness and timelessness and adapted to the contemporary spirit with changing glazes.

Seeking Beauty

Utility Objects in Finland

Liisa Räsänen

▶ *Kaj Franck,* Kilta, *1957–1975. Teema (Theme), 1981–*

Arabia and the Everyday Beauty movement

At the outbreak of World War II the Arabia Porcelain factory in Helsinki was the largest of its kind in Europe, and the majority of its products were exported. Its main products were dinner services and sanitary porcelain. After the war, Finland faced major changes. The refugees from the areas ceded to the Soviet Union, around 10% of the population, had to be resettled; Finland had to pay major war reparations; and there was a shortage of goods and materials in the country. An exhibition held by the Arabia art department at the NK department store in Stockholm took up the issue of utility design. Writing in the exhibition brochure, Carl Gustav Herlitz, director of the Arabia factory, notes that increased streamlining of production methods will provide more room for purely artistic creativity. The artist and designer must be given full freedom of expression within the bounds of available technology. "Thus art will not only be a flower worn on one's lapel, but something of deeper import."

In his review of the exhibition, Dr. Åke Stavenow, editor of *Form* magazine, acknowledged the high standards of Finnish design and applied arts, but also noted that good everyday utility objects did not attain the same level. He criticized the Arabia factory for focusing too much on art objects and for not having its artists participate in the design of utility objects. In this situation, they will easily become the flower in the lapel "which should be avoided in applied arts, because artistic ambition should be present in all areas of production". In his reply, Kurt Ekholm, artistic director of the Arabia factory, said that Stavenow was correct in noting that the designers on show did not work on utility objects, but asked why they should do so. "It is extremely questionable whether a strong and distinct artist personality can design utility objects, a task that requires at least as much knowledge of technology as artistic creativity." In connection with the reply, *Form* featured the comments of a number of Swedish ceramic designers on Arabia's separate departments for art and utility objects. Most of them regarded this division as a poor choice. The Swedish attitude was understandable. In 1919 the Swedish Society of Crafts and Design, Svenska Slöjdföreningen, had launched the "Everyday Beauty" (*Vackrare vardagsvara*) movement, which became a kind of idyllic predecessor of the Bauhaus in the 1920s. The Orrefors, Rörstrand, Karlskrona and Gustafsberg factories became widely known abroad through the efforts of the pioneers of the movement. Kaj Franck regarded the Swedish design of utility objects as representing good quality. The dinner services and tableware were restrained, studied, tastefully decorated and suited to the spirit of the Swedish welfare state. But the social atmosphere of Finland had always been more austere. During the 1930s Kurt Ekholm had been a protagonist of the Everyday Beauty movement at the Arabia factory, but the war ended these developments. There were also Finnish demands for more beautiful everyday objects. Commenting on an industrial fair held in 1947 Maire Gullichsen, a prominent figure in the design world, wrote a sharply worded review and a statement in favour of utility objects of greater aesthetic appeal under the heading "Utility Art Lost". Gullichsen asked what course industry will take when it regains its pre-war level of production. Will it continue as before? She noted that before the war Finland almost completely lacked everyday objects of beauty. "Factory salesmen, wholesalers and department stores think they know what the public wants. The present age calls for a 'democratization' of utility objects: we need articles of good quality at low cost."

The great challenge – The artistic design and democratization of utility objects

In November 1945 Kaj Franck began work as a product designer with the Arabia Porcelain factory. He found himself in an area of applied arts for which he had no training. Arabia wanted to renew its line of household tableware and Kaj Franck's task was to establish a design department for utility ware. Franck's initial impression of Arabia's large range of tableware was one of chaos. There were gilt-edged multi-part services decorated with decals and made according to European models and examples. But there were good, distinct utility objects. The collection, however, was marked by a certain superficiality, regardless of whether the example followed was Wedgwood, Meissen or Parisi-

Private Collection

Afternoon coffee in Viipuri in the home of Kaj Franck's grandfather Friedrich Franck at the beginning of the 20th century. At the table are Edvin, Friedrich, Allan and Erna Franck. Franck's father Kurt is standing and beside him are Linda Lydecken and grandmother Fanny Franck.

an ware. Franck felt that these services were a major challenge. "A radical solution to a social task seemed to be the only possibility. A functionalism challenging the undulating line and the Nordic idyll."

Changes in Finnish society also influenced Arabia. In 1946 the Finnish Population and Family Welfare Federation commissioned a dinner service which it would distribute free of charge to large rural families on social grounds. Franck's brief was to design this collection, which came to be known as the *Koti* (Home) service. Although consisting of a large number of items, this set of tableware excluded features unnecessary to dining, with the corresponding addition of dishes needed for cooking and storing foods, such as ovenproof casseroles. The service ultimately became a combination of various Arabia collections. By the end of 1947 some 40,000 *Koti* services had been made. A mug designed by Franck for *Koti* remained in production until the early 1970s.

Kaj Franck was also bothered by the sharp distinction between everyday objects and objects for festive use. Writing of his design principles in 1949, Franck noted:

"Couldn't something be done to that gilt-edged company of tableware? Yes, we could smash it. And break down the barriers between dinner services and unassuming kitchen and tableware... The present era must create its own idiom of form from the conditions and forms that belong to us... New materials and methods, and new needs, call for new solutions to the problems of form... There is no reason for compromise with the requirements of function."

"Tableware – Arabia's stepson?" This was the heading of Arthur Hald's interview with Kurt Ekholm in the January 1948 number of *Form*. Ekholm spoke of how the tableware department, founded two years previously, followed the principle of teamwork. The designers were given their assignments by a "design and model meeting" of representatives of the factory management, its sales and advertising departments, and artists. But owing to considerable difficulties in the availability of materials, among other problems, the results were not yet brilliant, but results could be expected in about three years. Ekholm was confident that separate departments for art objects and utility ware were the best solution. In the same number of *Form*, Ekholm described the current state of design and the existing shortage of goods and materials, rising prices and the housing shortage. Design played a minor role in such a situation. Of the various sectors of the applied arts, the furniture industry had suffered least. Ekholm was pleased that simple and functional design had been achieved in furniture, tableware, glass and ceramics.

Services – Tableware

The design of utility tableware at Arabia still interested Nordic industrial design circles. In a 1951 number of *Form*, Arthur Hald published a list describing the state of Finnish industrial design and design. According to him, the main problem of industrial design in Finland

Teemu Lipasti

A selection of Franck's cups and saucers from 1946–1973 on show at Artek 1979.

Y. Lintunen

Koti *service, RA 1946.*

was an imbalance between unbridled creativity and standard production. He noted, however, Kaj Franck's gradual progress in the design of utility ware. In 1951 Arabia's design and model meeting instructed Franck to design a set of tableware according to his own conception. This service, which became a collection of tableware, marked the beginning of a new era in the design of utility ware at Arabia. Franck set out by deconstructing the traditional concept of a dinner service. He first designed individual objects for a variety of uses. The individual objects became a set of tableware that was later given the name *Kilta*. The number of items was kept at a minimum, initially ten. The various items formed an adaptable entity that could be combined with other tableware.

The Wärtsilä group of companies, which owned Arabia, bought the Nuutajärvi glassworks in 1950. Kaj Franck became the designer, and its artistic director in 1951.

The new line of design adopted by Arabia and Nuutajärvi was on show in 1952 at Wärtsilä's recently opened showrooms, which had been designed by Franck. New features were the simple geometric forms of the objects, their compatibility and versatile use. Coloured glazes were the only decoration applied to the ceramics. The exhibition proved to be a success. This new design made a breakthrough at a tableware exhibition held in Copenhagen in early 1953. A local

Timo Kauppila

IS jars designed by Kaj Franck 1949–1952. In production they were 1953–1975.

newspaper described it as a "revolution at the dinner table".

An exhibition of new industrial design objects by Arabia and Nuutajärvi at the NK department store in Stockholm in 1954 was also a success. Gotthard Johansson of the newspaper *Svenska Dagbladet* commented:

"Kaj Franck, one of Arabia's leading designers, has recently devoted his efforts completely to the design of utility ware... creating a completely new range of simple utility objects... One can only applaud the achievements of Kaj Franck and his colleagues – Kaarina Aho, Saara Hopea, Ulla Procopé and Nanny Still – for creating simple, low-cost objects for use that are of pure and distinct form and consistent structure with a simplicity that is a natural and self-evident stylishness, of which we could learn a great deal."

Finnish tableware had become acceptable. Arabia and Nuutajärvi devoted effort to the presentation of products, information and marketing in order to make these aesthetically pleasing utility objects available to everyone. In 1956, the first number of *Keramiikka ja Lasi* (Ceramics and Glass), a magazine published by Arabia and the Nuutajärvi glassworks, instructed its readers: "...everything that now surrounds our everyday existence, i.e. most of our days and weeks, must give us the aesthetic satisfaction that each one of us yearns for, wittingly or unwittingly...".

Theme and *Team*

In the 1960s, Kaj Franck divided his efforts mainly between the Nuutajärvi glassworks and the Institute of Arts and Crafts in Helsinki. Although this meant less time for the design of ceramics, Franck managed to create a number of pairs of cups and condiment sets as well as hot-water and tea pourers and frying dishes from flame-resistant ware. Owing to technical problems, many objects that had been designed for many years, such as the *Lumipallo* (Snow ball) service and samovar, could not be produced. Kaj Franck noted in many connections how the special rhythm of glass fascinated him and how it suited him best.

Kaj Franck created a specific line for Nuutajärvi that began with coloured blown glass. In the 1960s he sought to achieve smoother, more lucid and thinner pressed glass and maximum refraction by developing techniques and the composition of the actual glass. Franck wanted to blur the boundaries between pressed and blown glass. The result was a series of twenty pressed-glass tumblers, beginning with *Puristelasi I* (Pressed Glass I) in 1953 and ending in *Delfoi* in 1976.

In many lectures and talks, Kaj Franck defined the criteria of aesthetically pleasing utility objects. "When talking of beauty we mean not only functionality and perfection of style but also in some cases timelessness as well. This expresses how greatly we appreciate the concept of beauty." In an interview, Franck once described the successful creation of a timeless glass design: "It was made with an automatic machine. It fitted one's hand, and it had a slight refractive effect owing to differences in thickness. It never made the Finnish market as a tumbler. It was made into a container for mustard and cheese spread. In that form, it found its way into many homes." The tumbler was named *Polo*.

Franck's last design assignment at Arabia was the redesign of the discontinued *Kilta* tableware to meet contemporary requirements. Named *Teema* (Theme), the new collection began to be produced in 1981 as a basic set of tableware for the home. The undecorated *Teema* collection can be combined with other tableware and materials. Kaj Franck wanted his objects to attach themselves to their environment in an unforced manner. He sought to dissolve the distinction between everyday articles and objects for festive use by creating universal objects for all kinds of use.

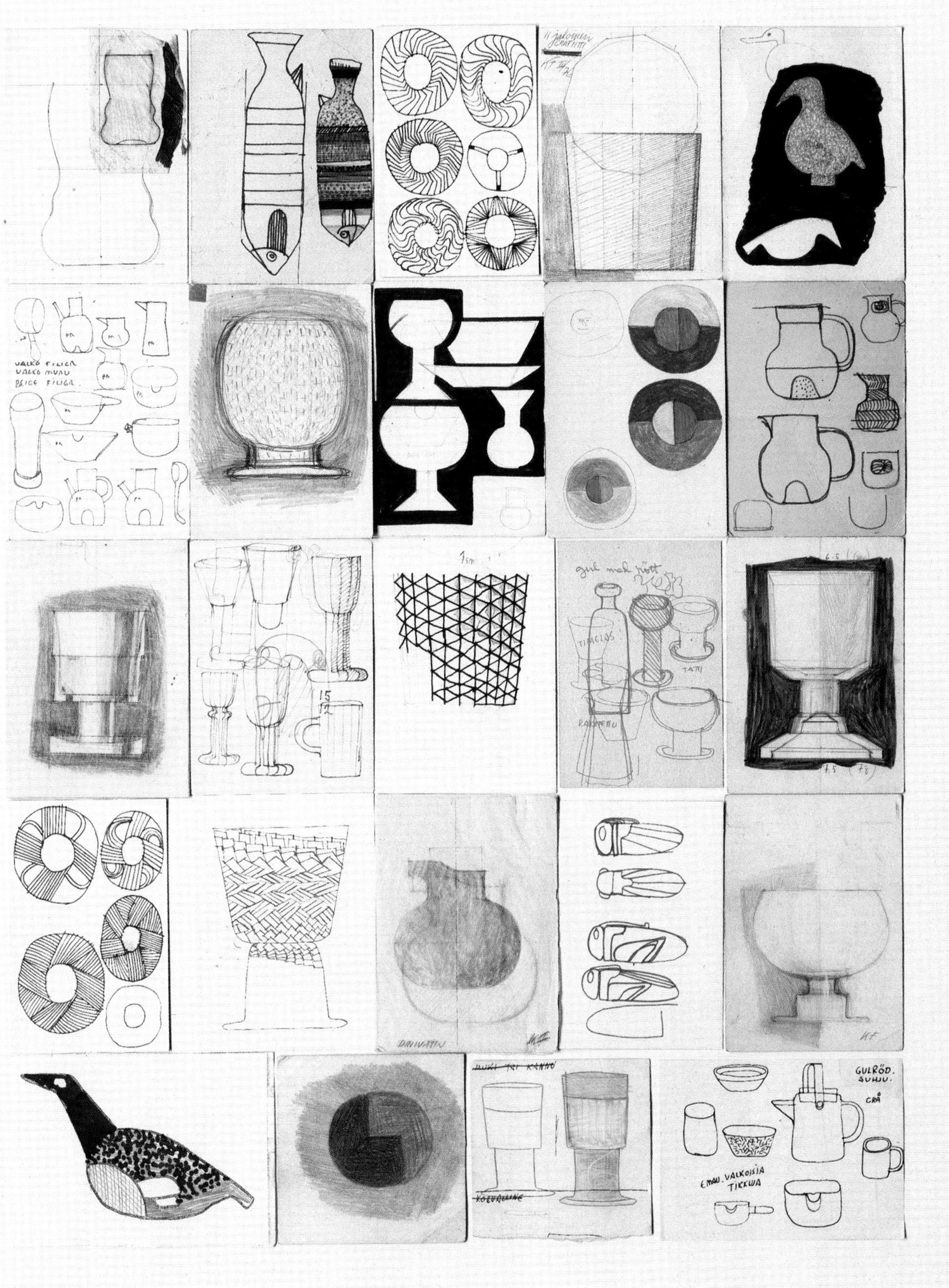

Sketches for glassware 1960–1976.

In the 1970s, Franck delivered an address on aesthetic facility and design at the University of Art and Design in Helsinki, quoting a poem by the Finnish poet Pentti Saaritsa:

"I was mixed up enough
To find the words.
Shame that the world is now such
That a poem can never be perfect anymore.
And what would be finished anymore.
A scream, a news item, a body count?
And all the papers,
Are posthumous papers."

Franck went on to observe: "*The environment consists of the reflections of all these, and earlier, times, even though each generation seeks to wipe out the traces of at least its immediate predecessors. An aesthetic appreciation of the environment is the prime requisite in industrial design, for the product of design is never alone. It is not on a stand or in a glass case, or in a frame… Instinct and its reverse face, experience, are aesthetic qualities, which I regard to be the starting point for aesthetic choice. It is impossible to distinguish the aesthetic component from the process of product design. Nor can it be added afterwards.*"

Liisa Räsänen archives

Casing glass beeing made. Kaj Franck and master glassblower Jaakko Niemi.

Jorma Puranen

The courtyard of the Ministry of Education. Designed by Lauri Anttila, Olli Tamminen and Kaj Franck.

Arto Hallakorpi

Filigree tumblers 1975–77.

Close to Nature

Carla Enbom

Light may well be the phenomenon characterizing the natural environment of the North. Light – its presence and absence. Although the long polar night of winter has its appeal, most people live from one summer to the next. The white nights are a fact – on the 17th of May the sun will rise in Northern Finland to remain above the horizon until the end of July. Despite all this, the return of the light feels just as wonderful each year. Silence – peace and quiet – can also have a profound effect. One notices it when it is broken. To hear the call of the diver over still water is an unforgettable experience. Here everyone loves his or her own landscape and the proximity of nature has a kind of inspiring effect on everyone.

Where the sun glows in vivid colours in the south, the northern light lends value, tinges and hues. Over the centuries a sensitive, subdued light, has shaped the Finnish spirit no less than the climate and the bare conditions of existence itself. An unassuming and simple style has been something self evident for most people in this borderland between east and west. Asceticism has been our strength and a good starting point – directness has defined our place in the world. New needs create new forms. The heritage of simplicity is also one of opportunity; it does not bind or restrict. We have not had to take note of meanders and vines that have "always" existed. Here, functional form has always taken precedence. Change has been slow and the functional aspect has been adopted from new styles. The legendary designer and teacher Kaj Franck taught a whole generation of students that the basis of solving all problems of design is the underlying need. The craftsman, the designer, must be led by necessity and he or she must respond to needs. To seek popularity is a shortsighted strategy.

A renaissance of arts and crafts

The Finns have been fortunate to have a rich tradition of crafsmanship and the opportunity to modify and pass on this tradition. The creator of things new falls into a continuous dialogue between the need to preserve and to renew – a desire to belong and the need to stand out. It is possibly the demand for the personal touch that justifies the craftsman's existence today. Gone are the days when a young man had to prove himself to his intended by carving her a distaff board, or for the fiancée to fill her bridal chest with home-spun linen. Today's crafts are bought, and fortunately there are still bearers of tradition finding pride and joy in the skills of the hand, and choosing to pass them on. The nostalgic line has been reinforced by an ecological justification for creating products that will last for generations.

Kristian Runeberg

Markku Kosonen. On the right is a detail of his sprouting willow basket.

Jussi Tiainen

The sheath-knife is a very personal artefact. Whether factory-made or forged by a blacksmith, it must fit in the user's hand and have the right feel.

There is a renaissance of crafts today. As a result of widespread unemployment, many municipalities invested in crafts education and training with the sincere hope that the new carpenters, weavers and potters would remain in their home regions, establish businesses in former industrial facilities and thus employ themselves. There are some 40 crafts schools in Finland today, and a national project has been launched to encourage local trends to underscore their individual nature.

In traditional perspective we may mention reedwork in Kruunupyy, straw crafts in the Porvoo region, Ostrobothnian weaves, and the wooden boxes and containers of the Uusikaupunki area. The boat builders of the coastal regions have traditionally been skilled carpenters and cabinetmakers. Many people in the coastal regions have also knitted woollen sweaters, according to disposition and skills, in bright colours or with simple designs and natural dyes.

Education has brought wood to the fore again. Cabinetmakers are an emerging group that are taking on the most demanding projects, a pleasing prospect in an area of craftsmanship that should be self-evident in Finland.

There is a justification and need for crafts, offering a touch that is not found in manufactured items. Roughly speaking, craftsmen can focus on two groups of customers: quality-conscious buyers interested in individual products of enduring value, and the impulsive buyer, or tourist. Souvenirs should preferably have a local or national connection, have some useful purpose and be durable. They should not take up room, be heavy or too expensive, and thus labour-intensive. Easier said than done.

Local materials

Traditional craftsmanship meeting these criteria is represented, for example, by Sámi (Lapp) crafts with products of reindeer antler and hides and masur, or curly, birch. These materials require special skills which have long traditions in Lapland. There is a heritage of insight of techniques and material, an unbroken tradition that lives on. The former necessities for survival involving the use of available material have now become an economic means of livelihood – crafts production for the tourist industry. Genuine Sámi crafts are attractive and desirable but by no means cheap. However, simple articles such as buttons made of antler correspond to most of the criteria of ideal souvenirs.

Production true to nature is often based on local materials – to dig where one stands. Just as potters would often establish themselves near a field with red clay, and glassworks were built near rich reserves of forest providing fuel for the furnaces. Birch bark is an interesting material in the national context. In the past, Finns living in the forests would make boxes, knapsacks and footwear out of birch bark. Folklore warns girls about young men who come courting with a ring of birch bark – the love will last only as long as the ring. Today, we see the opposite and bark may even have a chic image. One of Helsinki's leading pastry shops sells exquisite marzipan strawberries in small birch-bark boxes, like items from a 19th-century painting.

A beautiful fabric in the Museum of Art and Design in Helsinki is a weave of paper string and strips of birch bark, made by textile designer Greta Skogster-Lehtinen in 1942. Here, too, the result was dictated by necessity. Despite the crisis and shortage of materials of the war years, the designer was able to bring forth the beauty of simple materials. To speak of birch-bark crafts today has a certain condescending tone referring to peasant romanticism and an outmoded way of life, but the products themselves are still things of undeniable beauty.

Modern wood and bark crafts

Markku Kosonen took on the challenge of demonstrating the new possibilities and opportunities of much-neglected birch bark. The result was an array of freely shaped baskets with curling edges, as well as boxes and containers made in layers and laminated into a strong and durable construction. Often the answer lies between function and expression. His baskets of willow and bark have been pieces of living nature placed in galleries and glass cases. He once held an unforgettable Easter exhibition in which his baskets of freshly cut willow began to sprout leaves. It was a transient homage to the coming spring, while the Christian feast of Easter and death were noted with a circle of thorns.

Museum of Art and Design/Jean Barbier

Periferia Design/Rauno Träskelin

A beautiful example of organic fabric is a weave of paper string and strips of birch bark, made by textile designer Greta Skogster-Lehtinen in 1942.

A good example of the new use of bark: a stool by Simo Heikkilä 1999.

Another interpretation would be a massive layerdness as expressed in his laminated bowls and dishes.

Kosonen practices what he preaches. He feels that a craftsman or artisan should devote himself to what cannot be achieved industrially. Accordingly, catkins can remain on his baskets or the wildly sprouting branches may form a thick wreath. Here, a playful aesthetic is involved. Also the loose constructions of later times have become the archetypes of baskets. Kosonen is an example of how a craftsman can make a living from what he does. The most important things are not to stagnate, but to make use of opportunities and to market oneself both at home and abroad. Crafts are cultural communication.

Stone and silver

Silversmith Bertel Gardberg is another craftsman who has always been in his own category. This master of many materials has continually been inspired by the wealth and richness of nature. His works include direct adaptations of natural forms, such as a tern on a sugar spoon, boxes taking the shape of an apple core, or beetles and dragonflies of polished stone with details in silver that have become classics of Finnish crafts. Working with a confident eye and steady hand, Gardberg captures the character and shape of small creatures, enlarging them and presenting the complex constructions that make them function and survive. Despite their weight his butterfly profiles in polished black granite contain the whole essence of the butterfly and his stylized insect figures preserve the basic form of the model, as for example a firefly made of copper ore.

A true craftsman, Bertel Gardberg makes most of his tools himself. Being skilled in carving, he needs proper knives, and has designed three now industrially made models. These knives all meet functional and aesthetic requirements, even down to their handles ending in the heads of otters, seals or eagles.

Networking in crafts

Since not all craftsmen are able to work alone, various organizations offer their help to those with limited opportunities. Some of these organizations operate on a nation-wide basis, issuing publications, counselling and holding seminars, while others are regional in focus and able to engage in crafts activities at a more personal level. An example is an association whose name (Gullkrona) harks back to the Middle Ages.

According to legend, Queen Blanka of Sweden sailed through the Southwest Finnish archipelago on a voyage to Finland in the 14th century. On her way, she saw an expanse of open water so beautiful that she gave her golden crown to it, and named it Gullkrona (Golden Crown). The crafts association of the Turunmaa region named itself Gullkrona, a symbol of all that is good and beautiful in life. For almost 40 years this association, founded by a firebrand and still led in a spirit of enthusiasm, lends support to the crafts industries of the coastal region. It has the admirable aim of carrying on traditions, promoting crafts skills, and helping home industries market their products. Gullkrona has given many people in the archipelago an opportunity to earn extra income. For those living in the outer archipelago, without regular contact with the mainland – at the time of writing the ice is breaking and the isolation of the islands is at its worst – links with a domestic industry centre can be a veritable lifeblood.

Gullkrona relies on the enthusiasm and idealism that is the basis of all its work. Crafts are somehow able to rise above crass self-interest; they are borne by a living tradition and the freedom which it provides. Those who become part of this circle will feel pride in being able to make durable functional objects of beauty and work higher values than economic gain. Gullkrona follows the same principles today as when it was founded. It seeks to maintain high standards and to sell the products of its members in its own shops and at markets and trade fairs. In addition it counsels and holds courses for professional craftsmen, amateurs and children. Together with the craftsmen Gullkrona seeks to adapt traditional products, materials and techniques to modern requirements.

Jussi Aalto

Bertel Gardberg in his studio. On the right Damselfly: silver, larvichite and obsidian, 1988.

Jussi Aalto

Ari Rosila

The sea plays a prominent role in the archipelago, and in the present age of plenty consumers must be attracted with things that cannot be obtained elsewhere. The products of Gullkrona include sweaters with Viking ship designs, coasters of plaited rope suggesting the art of sail making, bottle-openers in the form of a wooden fish, scarves with schools of flounders, candelabras and lanterns of the same design as used in homes in the archipelago, and of course woven cloths, towels and rugs. The symbol of Gullkrona is a three-pointed crown that is also used in a gingerbread mould that is sold with a recipe created for it.

The sea has always provided more links than isolation. In this age of international cooperation, a new network, entitled Utmärkt skärgårdsslöjd (Excellent Archipelago Crafts) is being developed, extending from the Stockholm archipelago to the Åland islands and the Turunmaa archipelago. This organization is also seeking quality products made in the archipelago and associated with the seafaring heritage.

The Fiskars cooperative

Craftsmen can also collaborate in collectives of a single area or region. Fiskars, an industrial community in Southwest Finland, has created a functioning community of craftsmen, designers and artists in only a few years. When the Fiskars Group was reorganized, it was able to attract new inhabitants to its former houses for workers and vacated factory buildings, which have subsequently been restored to become studios and working space. This marked the end of a quiet life at Fiskars. Today, this village of 500 has a 65-member collective of craftsmen and designers – a high proportion of creative effort.

The richness and strength of the new cooperative lies in the variety of its members: carpenters, blacksmiths, potters, glass designers, textile designers, tool makers, instrument makers, paper makers, designers and artists. Cooperation is strength. A potter can order a wooden base for a vessel, an interior architect will design fixtures, and a cabinet maker can make it from the desired timber. Products are made in small series easily adapted to the needs of clients.

Since its founding, the cooperative has held group exhibitions that have become popular destinations for

Rauno Träskelin

outings. The fruits of the past winter's labours are put on show when early summer is in full bloom, and the success of past years has led to growing numbers of visitors, healthy sales, wide attention – and sponsors. A copperworking shop and a granary have been repaired through volunteer work to serve as exhibition venues. The cooperative has always wanted its products to represent a high standard of design and execution. New members are accepted only after discussion and deliberation, and an annual jury selected from among the members chooses the material for the an-

▲ *Interior of the old ironworks of Fiskars, where an international ceramics exhibition was held in the summer of 1998.*

Perttu Rista

nual exhibition. One example of a growing awareness of quality at Fiskars is the fact the plastic outdoor tables and chairs of a local pub have gradually been replaced with garden furniture made of oak.

Fiskars is an industrial community with old traditions, and its idyllic and beautiful setting inspires its craftsmen and attracts visitors. Over the centuries, hardwoods have been planted in the village and it is a point of honour for the carpenters of Fiskars to use from among the fifteen local timber species those that are not used by the furniture industry. Foliate forms and shapes can also be adopted in ceramics; a nut can inspire the shape of a bowl; and thin strips of bast can be torn from lime. On one occasion an artist had dyed sawdust in different colours and used it to make a temporary installation on the floor – to be swept away after the exhibition. Blacksmiths willingly follow the traditions of the old Fiskars ironworks. The hand-wrought sheath-knifes hark back to a time predating the orange scissors and modern axes of Fiskars.

Museum of Art and Design

Detail of a pattern called Sails by Sirkka Könönen.

In addition to the annual general exhibition, there are also exhibitions on special themes at Fiskars – wood, paper, ceramics etc. Foreign participants are often invited, a source of both challenge and impulses. Different materials attract different groups of visitors, and a variety of things being offered ensures continued interest. For example, a new feature last year was a garden exhibition with advice and counselling for visitors. The exhibits included a large range of plants, tools, implements, pots and outdoor furniture, for the pleasure and benefit of visitors and local summer residents.

► *Maisa Turunen-Wiklund's unraveled old paper string, which are twist,ed into new shapes and forms. The Shadows of* Vanamo.

Light and nature in textile design

Textile design relies on a solid tradition both technically and aesthetically. Finland's rich vernacular tradition of textiles has been developed and furthered not only at the Friends of Finnish Handicraft, but also in private companies, such as Kotivilla of Tammisaari. Of the craftsmen and artisans whose works are directly associated with nature, the following section presents textile designers, in whose oeuvre renewal and tradition are linked in various ways. These artists and designers express the moods of nature and the play of colour in various techniques and materials, but can still present forest or the sea as such.

The latter include for example Sirkka Könönen, whose knitwear revives the flora and fauna of Finland and who has succeeded in making an art from these everyday garments. One could well display sweaters designed by her when they are not worn. Influences and impulses from the wilderness environment of her childhood in Northern Karelia emerge in band and strip designs in her sweaters, with bears, reindeer and elk crossing bogs and forests, and the colours of crows, grouse and pheasants following each other and changing at the same pace as the seasons. Applying her absolute sense of colour, Könönen conjures forth richly nuanced hues in the rhythmic patterns of her garments. The themes may also be figurative. For example there is something humorous and endearing about her row of foxes with white-tipped tails marching along at the same pace, as in a mischievous fable or folktale. The whole is carefully considered and studied, with a balance of colours and images. Könönen works with confidence and command, continuing and developing old traditions. Combining different orientations in a rich way, she has created a unique style while promoting the emergence of a new wave of patterned knitwear.

Pliant paper

Nature is present in a similar way in the works of Maisa Turunen-Wiklund. These intimate pieces recreate – from paper alone – naturalistic blueberry twigs or tempting berries in a bark box. With endless patience, this artist unravels old paper string to glue, sew, twist, bend and straighten them into new shapes and forms. In her hands wreaths and bouquets turn into bunches of dried flowers. The simple Burnet rose grows against a twined green screen; autumn leaves fall on moss; and willow-herbs spread their curly down. Each petal is of the right size and colour and they are all found in the right numbers in the phylotaxes. The artist's haystacks, resembling the matted hair of angels, have found their way to museums. Delicate yet attuned to everyday life, her works have a quiet and illusorily vivid effect.

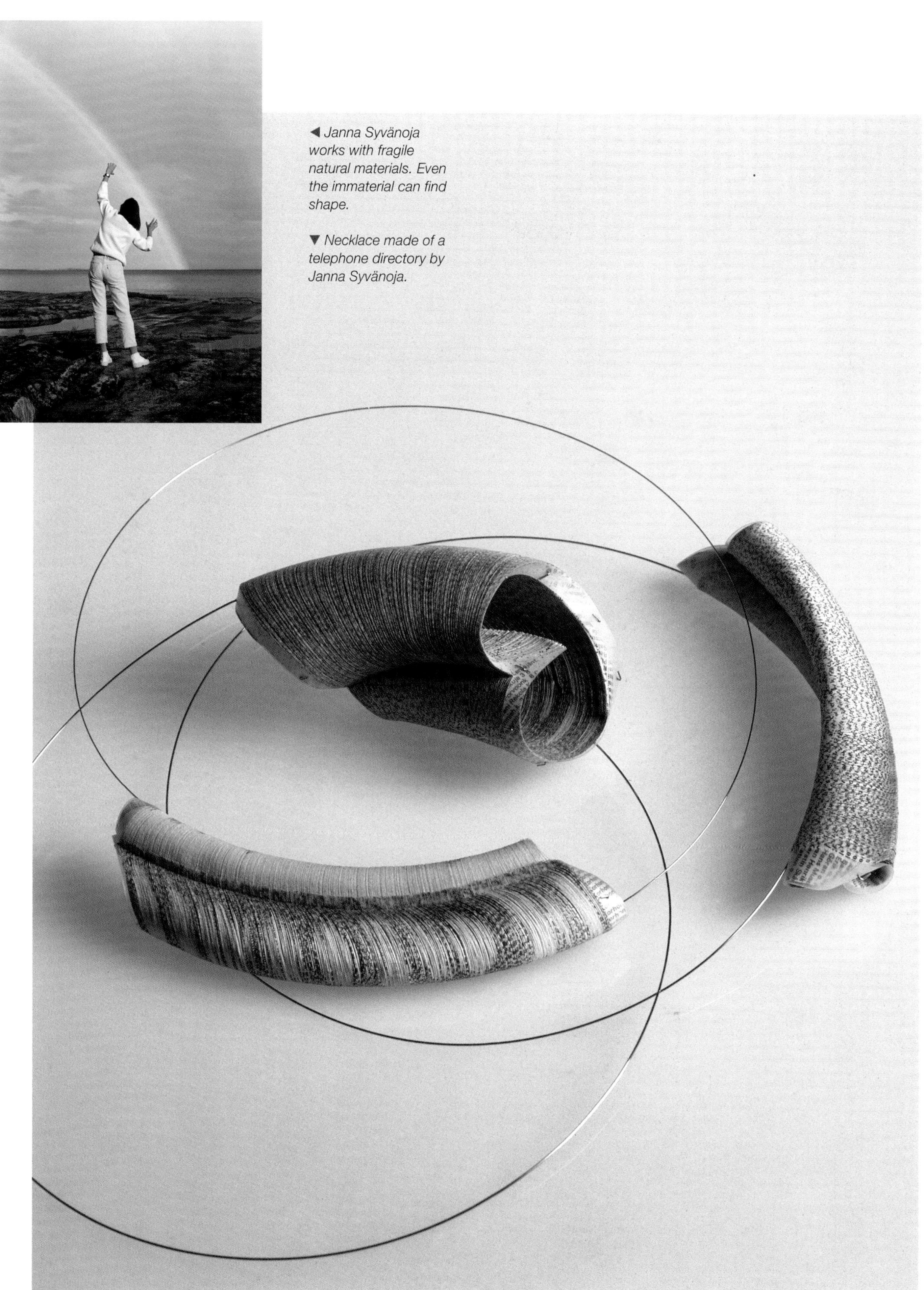

◀ *Janna Syvänoja works with fragile natural materials. Even the immaterial can find shape.*

▼ *Necklace made of a telephone directory by Janna Syvänoja.*

Ulla Hassinen

Maisa Turunen-Wiklund works in a slow and laborious technique. The whole is often formed of hundreds of minor details that must be combined. Once on a train Maisa Turunen-Wiklund knitted stitches from something vaguely greenish grey that was to gradually become a haystack. A fellow passenger finally asked her if she was quite sane. The artist replied that she often asked the same question herself, but pointed out that her mission in life was to explore all the possibilities of paper and thus bring nature into our lives.

Merja Winqvist represents a completely different kind of expression in her patient work with paper. She uses paper to make tubes which she glues, varnishes and paints. They almost have the strength of wood, their original form, but the new material is lighter and more pliant. Winqvist links her tubes and staffs of paper with flax into sculptural compositions. Their forms may be related to old hunting implements, boat structures, with long, stretched kayak-like shapes with something mythical about them. These pieces can well be hung in the air, revealing their delicate tones from different directions and letting their complex shadows come into their own. These works can also be regarded as an independent variant of the traditional Finnish straw mobiles of Christmastime, hung above the Christmas table in the warmth of the candles.

Janna Syvänoja is an artist expressing nature and its cycles in an extremely delicate and new way. Her exhibitions show how the immaterial can find shape and how she can capture the flight of time in a fragile and aesthetic way. Seeds falling to earth and joined with hair of the mane cast a shadow more real than the work itself. No less ethereal are her vase forms made of half decomposed leaves, with the contours formed by the veins. A worm-eaten sheet of paper with Japanese characters becomes a kind of travel diary, while the page of an old newspaper found in a demolished house finds a new life once it is put forth and framed. The traces of dreams on a pillowcase are marked with a hair.

It all began with Janna Syvänoja making jewellery from paper, using thin strips of paper cut from telephone directories and tightly bound with wire. The value of the jewellery is in their craftsmanship and artistic execution and not in their material. The pieces contain hidden messages, especially of an ecological nature. The technique itself tells of careful, time-consuming work.

Ever since the beginning of her career, Janna Syvänoja has raised, and fulfilled, considerable expectations. She works in a completely unique manner and spirit, and all her works have some purpose, message or insight. She has not let her considerable success lead her astray, but continues in the same unassuming yet profound vein in which she began. Janna Syvänoja has always defended her own independence: "My first years at the University of Art and Design were a time of passive rejection." Intuitively seeking her own course, she has the perception to set forth what most others do not see. She has deep respect for all the phenomena which she encounters and the essence of all the materials which she chooses.

No less attuned to nature is Maisa Tikkanen, working with a touch just as light and delicate in wool, her own material. Through trial and error Tikkanen has revised the techniques of felting, which has a long tradition in Finland. One's toes will never freeze in felt boots, no matter how cold it is. The felting technique came from the east. Itinerant Russians went from farm to farm, making felt boots from the wool of the farm. Maisa Tikkanen makes her works by laying long-fibred raw wool in layers, one colour next to the other, making the hues gradually change. The material is carded together, rolled tightly, and wet with hot water and alkaline detergent. The material is rolled and worked into a uniform mass, a soft felt of shiny, flaming colours. The result is a combination of tradition and creativity in which something deeply national has become universal, gaining increasingly freer forms of expression over time.

Similar subtle moods, though expressed in a completely different material, are found in Ulla-Maija Vikman's textiles. Vikman represents an exuberant textile-painting technique in freely suspended viscose thread. Shining strips of colour interrupted by horizontal elements create an abstract mood. The works are constructed with genial simplicity and create surpris-

Maisa Tikkanen lives in the heart of the Finnish lake district close to the Russian border. The variation of colour in her works reflects the changing of the seasons and the closeness of earth and water.

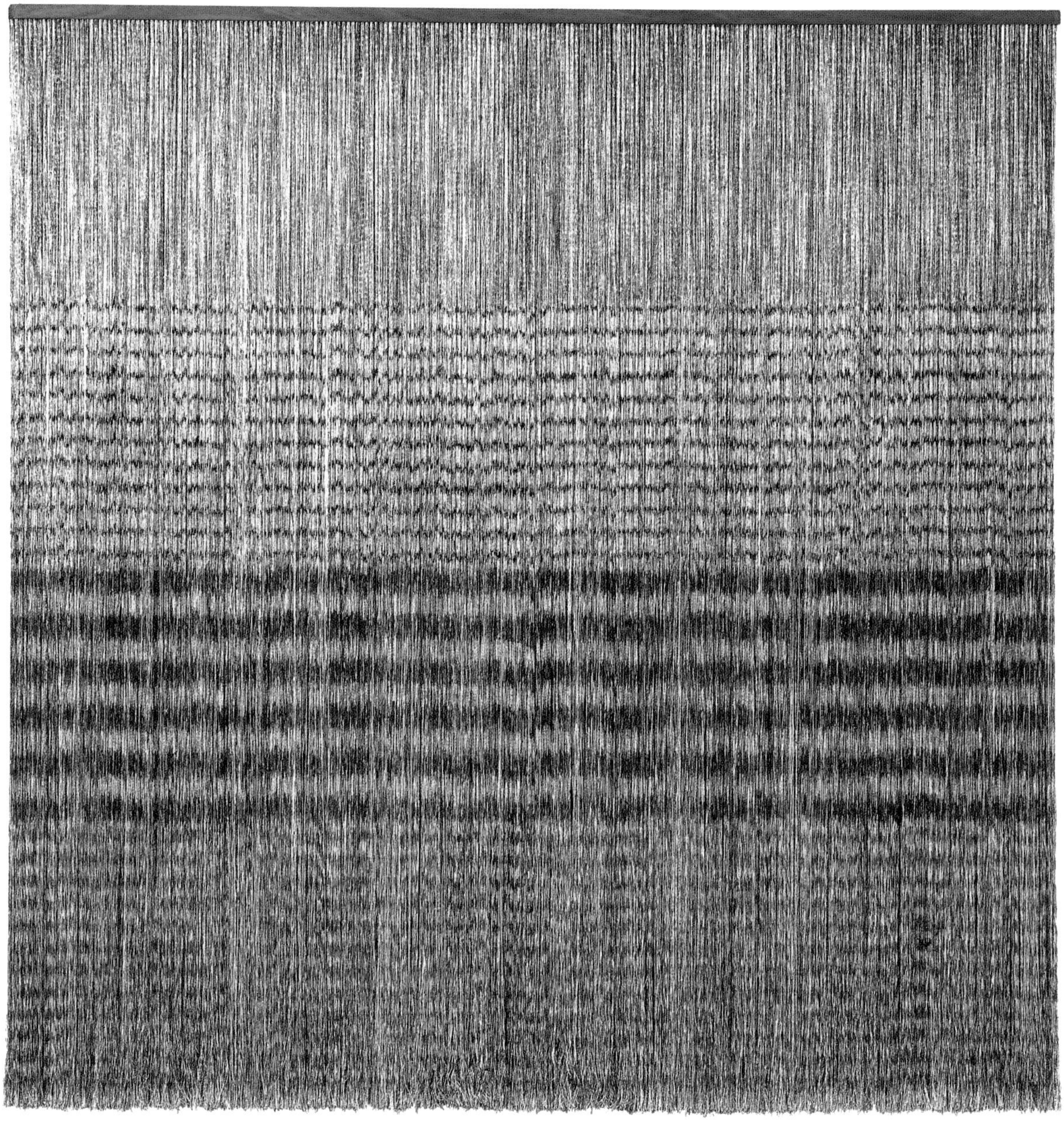

Design Forum Finland/Sameli Rantanen

Design Forum Finland/Sameli Rantanen

Ulla-Maija Vikman at work. Above the Bubo-Bubo *textile painting; viscose and linen. 180 x 180 cm, 1996.*

ingly beautiful effects. Vikman works by stretching bunches of thread on long tables. The threads are gradually painted in closely defined stages and then suspended from perforated bars or racks. An idea of what is involved here is given by the laconic title *47 km* (of thread) given to one of the works. The technique slightly resembles Indian ikat weaving, but with vertical warps, and with the reverse and obverse treated separately.

The impression made by these works is of a misty three-dimensionality, a surface with depth. A point of departure for this field of colour may be a view, against the light, of the bogs of Vikman's childhood, the open spaces of Northern Finland, or the feathery dress of the eagle owl (*Bubo bubo*). Light is important as a living element of all the works, continually changing in different kinds of light. Wikman's works are on show in many public buildings and facilities, for they are particularly well suited to different architectural environments.

Timber and paper are the backbone of Finnish industry, and the *ryijy* (*rya*) rug enjoys a tradition of seven centuries among vernacular textiles. Ritva Puotila's unique reliefs in ryijy technique partly combine both elements. Her material is paper string. Until the 1980s, when she began to experiment with paper, the older generation regarded paper as a wartime surrogate that was used for want of better materials. Ritva Puotila realized the possibilities and beauty of paper, and she has been responsible for making it almost fashionable.

Ritva Puotila's career had an ideal start when she received a gold medal for her ryijy weave at the Milan Triennials. This was in 1960, the year when she finished her studies in design. Her experiments with paper have led to serially produced mats and interior decoration materials, and to unique pieces of various colours. Where the manufactured items are unostentatious and even subtly elegant in their restrained colours, the unique textiles are derived from nature in very tangible and concrete terms.

Paper, made from wood fibre, is a living natural material, flexible, strong and solid. In Puotila's reliefs the tuft, up to 25 cm long, rises to form a living surface. The effect of height and depth is also achieved with a play of light and dark colour. A bright sun-yellow surface may suddenly take on an autumn hue, gradually fading the red glow. Puotila's colours can be indirectly described as seasons. According to her, bare early spring is the colour of potato peel, while November is dressed in a dark veil.

The attitude of Finnish craftsmen, artisans, designers and artists towards nature is perhaps best illustrated by a celebration of interior architect Simo Heikkilä's birthday. The organizers had agreed that artist friends from different fields would each make a bird box in honour of Heikkilä. A three-day exhibition was held, during which the public could admire a cavalcade of happy creativity, fifty bird boxes made in jest and in complete seriousness. There were soft textile boxes, nets that would hardly keep out the rain, "stone houses" of ceramics, shelves, brass fortresses immune to both cats and squirrels, creations of glass and paper, nests small and large, works of art with a message and instructions. Standing out among the presents was Markku Kosonen's large bird box of plaited willow tousled like Heikkilä himself.

These unique works, few of which could be placed in a birch in the yard, were finally auctioned. The proceeds went directly to the conservation of the shore lark (Eremophila alestris). This was a multidisciplinary happening and a unique homage to a popular interior architect and to Finnish nature.

Ritva Puotila, Woodnotes *carpet woven paper string. New York design.*

Woodnotes

Modern Fashion Design in Finland

Anne Veinola

At best, modern Finnish garments are like modern Finnish design in general: practical, unadorned, created more for everyday use than for festive occasions, and available to and usable by all. How has such a situation been achieved?

The history of the Finnish clothing is a tale of small businesses, innumerable bankruptcies and perseverance. Somewhat surprisingly, it is also a long history. Behind the business mergers, acquisitions and new names are often decades of work in the clothing and textile industry beginning with the early manufacturing establishments. People have always needed clothes, and in Finland the early broadcloth, woollen and cotton mills were trailblazers of industrialization.

Traditionally, clothing was made at home, or ordered. Underwear, overcoats, military apparel, and men's suits and shirts were already sewn semi-industrially in Finland towards the close of the 19th century. There were few imports and the ready-to-wear industry did not properly come under way until the middle of the 1950s, after the post-war period of shortages and rationing. Well into the 1960s, garments were ordered from seamstresses and tailors, and there were naturally recognized dressmakers and tailors in the towns and cities. The newspapers wrote of dresses and evening gowns created by Riitta Immonen, Kaarlo Forsman, Mauri Koponen and Irja Palonen and worn by the first ladies, beauty queens and movie stars. The style, however, was international, with Paris as the prime example. There was hardly any "Finnish" style. Finnishness in clothing mainly implied vernacular features and ornament, and except in knitwear their use was limited.

A change, however, already took place at the very beginning of the 1950s, led by Marimekko. In May 1951 a fashion show was held to present bold new uses for the fabrics of a textile printing firm known as Printex. The firm was owned by Viljo Ratia, husband of Armi Ratia of Marimekko. The prints were created by the recently graduated designer Maija Isola and from 1953 by Vuokko Eskolin-Nurmesniemi, with Armi Ratia as arbiter in matters of taste. The clothing for the first fashion show was designed by Riitta Immonen.

The show presented something totally unprecedented. The viewers were treated to clothing that was colourful, young, carefree and anything but the reversed, reworked and remodified wear of the years of shortage. The new clothing was made industrially – albeit originally in very small numbers. The names were also new: *Tik-Tak*, *Saunapolku* (Sauna Path), *Pomeranssi* (Bigarde), *Juhannusaatto* (Midsummer Eve), *Harlekiini* (Harlequin). The stylized floral patterns and broken colours of the 1940s had directly given way to the graphic designs and bright colours of contemporary art. The press and the public showed interest, and Marimekko came under way.

The new concepts of fashion gradually gained ground during the 1950s. Youth fashion emerged, at the time modelled after the blue jeans, leather jackets, Audrey Hepburn style and ballerina slippers familiar from American films. Marimekko and modern Finnish clothing made their breakthrough in the international market and among the international fashion-conscious public towards the close of the decade. In 1957, the first Marimekko fashion show was held in Stockholm and in 1960 the rest of the Western Hemisphere was conquered. Jacqueline Kennedy, who was the wife of the presidential candidate at the time, bought seven Marimekko dresses for holiday wear. This was given a great deal of publicity, and suddenly everyone wanted to know more about Marimekko, its designs, and Finnish clothing in general.

The emergence of modern "Finnish" clothing coincided with the triumph of Finnish design and architecture in the 1950s. Kaj Franck's *Kilta* service, Timo Sarpaneva's *i* glassware, Ilmari Tapiovaara's chairs and Alvar Aalto's architecture in brick had all presented features that would be associated with Finnish design: a command of the specific characteristics of material, studied proportion, natural materials, and an egalitari-

▶ *The* Jokapoika *shirt is an example of how a basic piece of clothing is moulded into a Marimekko look. Over 400 colour combinations have been used in the Piccolo material originally designed by Vuokko Nurmesniemi in 1953.*

an ethos of design for everyone. These same features became markedly prominent in the design of clothing and textiles for various uses.

Marimekko's success through its original and personal type of design made many others follow its example, and the design clothing concept was created. In 1964 the Kestilä company ordered the design of a collection of menswear from Timo Sarpaneva, and his wife Pi Sarpaneva designed a similar collection for women. Elina Kokkila and Rohdi Heintz of Sweden made coats for the Teiniasu company under the Dixi-Coat label, and the Finn-Flare autumn collection of 1964 was created by Maj Kuhlefelt (clothing design) and Marjatta Metsovaara (fabrics). Among the specialities of the period were the so-called *Ambiente* fabrics developed under the direction of Timo Sarpaneva. Dyed throughout with a special technique, their intense, glowing colours merged and blended with each other. Pi Sarpaneva designed coats and gowns in the *Ambiente* fabrics. Vuokko Nurmesniemi left Marimekko and in 1964 she established her own company, known as Vuokko.

During the 1960s and '70s intellectuals and self-styled progressives, who were generally interested in design and new trends, dressed either in Vuokko or Marimekko designs. For many years, male architects had as their uniform a Vuokko corduroy suit, a Marimekko *Jokapoika* shirt and a briefcase or satchel of thick cotton designed by Ristomatti Ratia for the Decembre company. But clothes were naturally designed and made elsewhere, too. Many of the leading names of the 1990s started their careers in the clothing industry: Ritva-Liisa Pohjalainen with the Piretta company, Marja Suna with Silo, Ritva Falla with Tiklas and Kestilä, and Jukka Rintala at Friitala, just to mention a few. Outdoor wear, one of the special areas of the Finnish clothing industry, also emerged. Torstai Oy, owned by Ritva and Jaakko Kellokumpu, was founded in 1974 to make skiwear. The Luhta company began to market its collections with the aid of top names in sports, and a motorcyclist's suit designed by Jasmine Julin-Aro for the Rukka company received an honorary mention in the Pro Finnish Design Awards of 1993.

But there were also critical comments. Why do the ladies always wear printed cotton dresses, even in the evening or at official dinners? "Printed colourfulness has been suitably matched by a measure of monochrome design," wrote Sirkka Vesa-Kantele of Finnish spring fashions in 1969. "Abroad, printed cotton dresses are sometimes regarded as a uniquely Finnish style."

The decades that followed were a golden age of exports for the clothing industry. Finnish clothes were sold in both the East and the West. Quality was the main consideration, but also labour costs were lower than in many other countries. Marimekko and Vuokko were the figureheads, while the large series of garments were made in many factories and companies all over the country.

During the 1960s Marimekko represented the avant-garde, and in the 1970s it stood for egalitarianism and soft values. The company produced peasant-type shirts, bright overalls, loose-fitting straight dresses, and striped cotton men's shirts with tin buttons. The patterns varied from architectural graphics to abundant Byzantine ornament. Basic colours or deep, broken hues were applied, and there were unexpected combinations of colours that often broke with established convention. Marimekko was much more than just a company producing printed fabrics and tricot clothing – it was a whole ideology. Over the years, its patterns and designs have come to decorate tin cans, tumbles, cloth slippers, raincoats, notebooks, coffee mugs, sheets and trays. There were even plans for a Marimekko Village, for which the architect Aarno Ruusuvuori designed an experimental house in 1967.

In accordance with its original principles, Marimekko has never been afraid to employ renowned designers who have often gained their reputation in completely different fields. Vuokko Nurmesniemi was originally a ceramist and Maija Isola was also a painter. Leading names of the 1990s in the design of printed fabrics include the graphic designer Marjaana Virta, the ceramist Fujiwo Ishimoto, the architect Antti Eklund, and the interior architect and sculptor Stefan Lindfors.

Where Marimekko concentrated on simplified design and reduced forms for basic items of clothing, shirt blouses, knitwear, trousers and jackets – and their reinvention, Vuokko made a sculptural entity out of the fabric and the moving human body. Evening gowns by Vuokko were not only brilliantly photogenic on the pages of magazines but also a cause celebre at fashion shows. Admittedly, they required their wearers to have posture, courage and height.

Vuokko Nurmesniemi was one of the first designers to reject the difficult pleatings, shaped drapery, buttons, hooks, linings and paddings of women's clothing. Zippers, rubber bands and pressed buttons replaced the former features and created a new aesthetic for the dresses and gowns. Alongside basic clothing of simple, reduced forms, Vuokko also designed almost unique items of clothing based on drapery, demanding cut and the properties of the fabric itself. Her many international awards and prizes show that Vuokko Nurmesniemi's special quality was also recognized elsewhere.

The profitability and economic viability of the clothing industry rapidly deteriorated towards the close of the 1980s. Exports to the former Soviet Union collapsed

◀ *After working as a designer with Marimekko, Vuokko Nurmesniemi founded her own company, named Vuokko, in 1964. Originally trained as a ceramist, Nurmesniemi is known for her ample, markedly sculptural and graphic dresses and gowns. The* Joki *dress from 1968, Vuokko.*

and labour costs rose. Bankruptcies followed each other in rapid succession. Finnish clothing had become too expensive, and foreign fashions exerted a greater appeal.

After thorough renewal and restructuring, the Finnish fashion industry began to rise again after the mid-1990s. The standard of workmanship and design was again underlined, and the products were aimed at the most important sector of the clientele, fashion and quality-conscious professional women. The first collections named after their designers were introduced on the market: the ril's collection by Ritva-Liisa Pohjalainen of the L-Fashion Group and Marimekko's Ritva Falla collection. Marja Suna was presented to the public as Marimekko's knitwear designer, and Jukka Rintala's studio-made evening gowns became a concept in their own right. Teri Niitti designed the Protesta collection for men, which was the subject of much interest. Many other designers presented their own small collections. Suddenly, there was again interesting Finn-

Best known for her knitwear, Marja Suna designed clothing for Marimekko in 1999. The Pisarat *(Raindrops) coat, silk and polyurethane, Marimekko 1999.*

Marimekko/Ari Lyijynen

ish clothing on the market. These products had high quality, studied cut and bold form and materials in common.

Armi Ratia had a vision that gave world fame to Finnish clothing design, at once traditional and radically new. Vuokko Nurmesniemi, on the other hand, regarded clothes as a scultural frame for the human body. Annika Rimala had the idea of clothes for all, which in the form of the striped T-shirt was spread all over the world in the thousands. Ritva-Liisa Pohjalainen, Ritva Falla, Teri Niitti and many others entertain the vision of high-quality, elegant Finnish clothing, adding a touch of luxury to everyday life. At the Department of Fashion and Textile Design at the University of Art and Design Helsinki, the students, the still anonymous designers of the future, have a vision of completely new forms, materials and ways of using clothing, not only to protect and cover the body, but also as a reflection of one's personality at the turn of the millennium.

Throughout the 1990s Jukka Rintala has been Finland's leading name in the design of evening gowns. The Karjalanmarja *costumes, cashmere, Marimekko*

Marimekko

Stripes forever

In the early 1970s you saw them wherever you went in Finland – in the city and at holiday homes in the country, in kindergartens and at rock festivals, worn by ordinary mothers, design-conscious people and the rebellious young. Jacqueline Kennedy had one. The young Princess Caroline of Monaco had one. I too had one, like both of the unisex-aware couple who lived next door. "It" was, of course, the Marimekko striped T-shirt.

Today the *Tasaraita* shirt is 30 years old. It stirred a furore when it was designed for Marimekko by Annika Rimala in 1968. She wanted to create a classic top to go with Levi's jeans and the original version was a brightly coloured, knitted cotton T-shirt with narrow stripes. The idea grew from there, and the first collection included not only short- and long-sleeve T-shirts but also a miniskirt, underwear and socks. The base colour for all of them was white at first, with bright red, blue, yellow and brown as the other colours.

The first *Tasaraita* collection sold out immediately in Finland. Output was stepped up and the market soon expanded to Scandinavia, the USA and continental Europe. The basic idea behind the concept – simplicity, clear colours and a fit for all kinds of people – was very Nordic in its precepts. In America it stood for fresh, European design, although it had points of contact with traditional design there, while in continental Europe it represented a trendily avant-garde, truly democratic way of dressing.

The basic concept of the T-shirt was subsequently applied to a very wide range of products – various skirts and trousers, nightshirts and underwear, cloth bags, bedding and towels, coffee mugs and memo pad covers – or postage stamps. In a book of postage stamps featuring Finnish design, in 1998, the Marimekko striped T-shirt is shown in such illustrious company as designs by Kaj Franck and Alvar Aalto. There have been dozens of colour combinations, both with white and featuring combinations of different colours. As always, the *Tasaraita* T-shirt is for women and men, adults and children. Mostly they have been made of a strong cotton knit fabric that lasts and lasts, ultimately finding an honourable use as a cleaning rag or worn for gardening or redecoration work.

Marimekko

Annika Rimala's Tasaraita *striped tricot shirts.*

When she designed the garment thirty years ago Annika Rimala was already known as a clothing designer and she had received recognition even outside Finland. Her aim was to make clothes that were timeless, practical and simple and which would suit people of all ages and sizes. Although it was meant to be merely a top to go with jeans, the striped shirt concept, which became almost the hallmark of Marimekko, became a fashion classic which still sells today in constantly changing colour combinations and new variant garments.

From Weave to Fibre

Päikki Priha

Folk textiles in museums demonstrate the high aesthetic and technical skills of Finnish women over the past centuries. Textiles for everyday use and wear were made in the home, a task almost automatically belonging to farmwives, who would pass on their skills to their daughters following a principle of apprenticeship. Towels of fresh colours, tablecloths, everyday wear, scarves, mats and covers were all made on the handloom in the home. The more valuable textiles for festive use, which were also a measure of the wealth of the household, were often made by itinerant weavers, who would also pass on their skills to the daughters of the house while the latter assisted them. It was a point of honour to have a large and well-made trousseau, and the daughters would decorate their own storerooms with their items.

The most valuable textile was the *ryijy*, or rya, rug. The most impressive ryijys, with tuft on both sides, were made for wedding ceremonies in the late 18th and early 19th century. On one side of the rug was long, monochrome tuft or pile originally meant to keep the person sleeping under it warm. The top side was decorated with shorter tuft forming a rich and colourful design. This side was kept on show when the ryijy was spread out on a bed.

▶ *A detail of Johanna Vuorinen's ryijy rug called* Juhlat *(Party). It won a ryijy competition declared in honour of the 80th anniversary of Finland's independence. The materials are wool and light fibre.*

Textile designers in the nunnery

Long before these ryijy rugs were made, there was a chronologically brief and geographically limited period attesting to unique aesthetic and textile-making skills of Finnish women. During the 15th and 16th centuries, a Brigittine convent, founded in 1438, operated in the town of Naantali on the west coast of Finland. Alongside other duties, the sisters had to make textiles for their home church – "to embroider with silk, gold and pearls the cloths needed to adorn the church and for the glory of God". Although only ten or so textiles made by the nuns have survived, they point to skills in various techniques, in both weaving and needlework. Although the designs mostly came from the Brigittine Order's main convent at Vadstena in Sweden, they were modified by their makers, thus giving the finished pieces a unique touch. In Finland, the convents and monasteries died out in the late 16th century, but textile crafts have lived on among the people, and beyond the monastery walls.

The threat of industry

The industrial revolution of the 19th century was a threat to native and popular handicraft. Imitations of European styles and mass-produced articles spread to Finland, raising concern about the deterioration of popular taste and the loss of crafts skills. The ideal of preserving national identity included the collection of vernacular textiles, the copying of their designs and patterns, and their renewed use. The Friends of Finnish Handicraft association was established in 1879 to maintain and promote crafts. It was modelled after the *Handarbetets Vänner*, or Friends of Handicraft, founded in Sweden in 1874. In her writings, the artist Fanny Churberg, one of the founders of the Friends of Finnish Handicraft, urged Finnish women to make use of the collected designs in their textile crafts. This was soon seen in the replication of folk ornament in all kinds of interior textiles, from sofa cushions, door and window curtains, tablecloths and seat covers to mats.

The Iris Room and the Flame ryijy

The beginning of the new era of Finnish textile design is often dated to the Paris World Fair of 1900, for which

the artist Akseli Gallen-Kallela prepared the interior design of the so-called Iris Room of the Finland pavilion. This included textiles which received a great deal of attention. A new feature was the use of tapestry technique in a wall frieze of a willow grouse, and its composition as an asymmetrical "bench ryijy". It was hung on the wall but also covered the seat and extended onto the floor. This "Flame" ryijy became a standard favourite in textile design, whose demand seems to live on through the decades. The Iris room was an exceptional example of a visual artist moving into textile design. Professional weavers and sewers carried out the work according to sketches and designs. This had been customary in European tapestry studios for centuries, but had not been adopted in Finland.

▶ At the beginning of the 20th century Finnish architects and artists also designed textile patterns. Eliel Saarinen's Ruusu *ryijy from 1904 is still a great favourite.*

As the importance of artistic design was recognized, a new period began in the work of the Friends of Finnish Handicraft, which had made the Iris textiles. The example of Gallen-Kallela encouraged architects and visual artists to test their designer skills in textiles, and to participate in the many design competitions held by the Friends of Finnish Handicraft. For some this happened only once, but for example the artist Väinö Blomstedt was the Friends' regular artist designer for two years, working on ryijy rugs, tapestries, drapes, pillows etc. Although the "textile designers" of the early 1900s were mostly men, this area was soon taken over by women.

Women to the Fore

The 1920s saw the emergence of a group of women textile designers with versatile training, capable of designing and realizing their designs, made either in series or individually. Eva Anttila, Greta Skogster, Laila Karttunen and others had received their basic design education at the Institute of Arts and Crafts, but had learned to weave at the Fredrika Wetterhoff School in Hämeenlinna. The artistic creativity of this new profession of textile designers followed the spirit of the times, even in comparison with other countries. The teachings of the Bauhaus seemed to have been taken for granted, and contemporary visual art tried its best to keep apace of textile design. When the Department of Textile Design was founded at the Institute of Arts and Crafts in 1929, the profession's first pioneering generation was already professionally active. Some of its members were to become the teachers and examples of future textile designers. Domestic contests and international expositions in Barcelona, Milan, Brussels and Paris in the 1920s and '30s encouraged the profession to ever improving achievements.

During the 1930s the industrial manufacture of textiles gradually became the domain of Finnish designers. The textile mills had already renewed and automated their machinery in the 1910s, but the designs came from Central Europe, and sometimes the design masters themselves. Dora Jung began her career in the 1930s as a designer of cotton damasks for the Tampella textile mills, the first manufacturer to hire a Finnish designer. The hand printing of fabrics that began in the 1930s had considerable impact on the development of print fabric design in Finland. It also provided employment for gifted designers. Among others, Eva Taimi and Kaj Franck designed fabrics for the *Taidevärjäämö* (Art Dyeing) company.

Before the second world war, most interior textiles were still woven by hand. The domestic furniture industry made almost exclusive use of them, thus offering work for several small hand weavers. The proportion of textiles woven at the Friends of Finnish Handicraft grew considerably throughout the 1930s, when textile designer Laila Karttunen was head of the Friends' weaving department.

The 1930s were a bright and unrestrained period in Finnish textile design. The ryijy rug was given a new, modern appearance. After being used on benches and on the floor it was again hung on the wall as a work of art. Ryijys by Impi Sotavalta, Toini Nyström and others reflect features of both Cubism and Functionalism. Eva Brummer was inspired by folk ryijys, but her search for examples had led her much further than other designers of the 1920s who had discovered folk ryijys. Brummer's designs combine religious feeling with primitive pagan strength and exuberance.

Another reformer of ryijy design was Uhra Simberg-Ehrström, who rejected patterns and created refined

The Friends of Finnish Handicraft used to collect and copy patterns used by people in the past and they were incorporated into new textile patterns. These patterns were also exchanged with the Swedish Handarbetets vänner organization.

The Friends of Finnish Handicraft

The Friends of Finnish Handicraft

Museum of Art and Design/Pietinen

▲ *Eva Anttila began making tapestries in the 1920s, working in this genre for over 60 years. One of her earlier works is* Primavera *inspired by Botticelli's painting.*

► *Dora Jung, a virtuoso of damask weaving. Birds were her favorite theme. Her work* Hässelby, *1976, is in Hässelby castle in Sweden.*

Museum of Art and Design

and subtle parallels of matching planes of colour. The depth and warm glow of the ryijy rugs was achieved by mixing threads of different hue among the pile and by not cutting the rows of pile to the same length. The result was the "value ryijy".

Tapestries and wall-hangings were also popular items of interior design. Eva Anttila began making tapestries in the 1920s, working in this genre for over 60 years. Maija Kansanen and Margareta Ahlstedt-Willandt were known as sensitive narrative tapestry designers. Hair carpets were a distinct area of design, being made for both private homes and public interiors, including the Parliament House in Helsinki.

The mother of invention

The second world war affected the material resources of textile designers. The lack of raw material did not, however, stem creativity but led to many innovative ideas. Surrogate materials included paper and paper string, from which mats, upholstery fabrics, garments and wallpaper were woven. When the ground fabric was not available, curtains and tablecloths were printed on crêpe paper. The products were practical as well as aesthetic.

A beginning for new things

A new era and style followed the war. It now seemed as if the forced interruption of creativity had expanded the range of designs and colours in textiles. The 1950s have been described as the decade of success for Finnish design and industry, with reference to acclaim and prizes obtained at many international exhibitions. Bright-coloured fabrics with large designs were made by Marimekko, founded by Armi Ratia in 1951. Marimekko's first designers included Vuokko Eskolin-Nurmesniemi and Maija Isola.

Hand-woven interior textiles were replaced with industrially manufactured series, many of which became classics of Finnish textile design. Even today, there would be demand and use for the timeless interior fabrics of Kirsti Ilvessalo, Rut Bryk and Uhra Simberg-Ehrström.

The 1950s also saw the rise of art textiles. Examples of international recognition in this field included the many prizes and awards received at the Milan triennale. Recognized and fêted designers included Kirsti Ilvessalo, Eva Brummer, Dora Jung, Laila Karttunen and Uhra Simberg-Ehrström.

The expansion and growth of textile design led to the founding of the TEXO Textile Designers association in 1956, operating in connection with the Finnish Association of Designers ORNAMO.

The activities of the 1960s concentrated on industrial design, for which students of textile design at the Institute of Arts and Crafts were trained under Eliisa Salmi-Saslaw from 1963. Kirsti Rantanen began to teach print design in the early 1960s, with the emergence of a new freelancer group of textile designers as a result. In addition to colourful prints, woven fabrics also became very popular. Marjatta Metsovaara's interior textiles were fascinating creations in terms of colour, material and their new types of binding. In Northern Finland, Elsa Montell-Saanio revived the traditional Lapp *raanu*, a shaggy coverlet, in a new and fresh manner. Design textiles – ryijy rugs, raanu weaves, double cloth weaves and tapestries – figured prominently alongside industrially manufactured woven and printed fabrics.

Museum of Art and Design/Jan Alanko

Uhra Simberg-Ehrström could use ryijythreads like the artist uses his palette. It looks as if Neljä väriä *(Four colours) consists of four colours but in fact 70 threads of a different hue have been used. Friends of Finnish Handicraft, 1956.*

Bold-coloured printed fabrics with large designs were spread on tables and beds, hung on walls and used as curtains. Prints had come to stay. In 1974 Fujiwo Ishimoto of Japan came to work for Marimekko. Alongside many dramatic and startling designs, Ishimoto has also created a large number of quiet and gently restrained fabrics in which basic Japanese forms have found a Finnish interpretation.

Hennika, *a printed fabric designed for Marimekko by Vuokko Nurmesniemi in 1957.*

International trends in the 1970s

The energy crisis and recession of the 1970s also affected the Finnish textile industry. As cheap imports burgeoned, the domestic textile industry receded. In the 1970s the Finnish designer was no longer a fêted artist but an anonymous servant of industry bowing to the demands of machinery and international trends. Architecture discarded textiles from interior design, replaced walls with windows and placed more value on cast concrete than on works of art. "Is there any room for design textiles?" asked Annikki Toikka-Karvonen with concern in 1971. Writing in *Arkkitehti,* the Finnish Architectural Review, in 1977 the art critic Erik Kruskopf noted: "Rarely can one see design textiles and an architectural environment together as a studied and considered whole." The workshop concept began to interest not only potters and ceramists but also textile designers. Workshops for one or a few persons began to be established in deserted laundries and garages. Their products were sold at Artisaani and Pilkku, crafts cooperatives in Helsinki. The model for the new craftsmanship was taken from Sweden, while the themes and motifs came from the east. Russian ornament and the motifs of East European storybooks appeared in gaily-coloured prints by the *Painopaja Puolukka* and *Pohjan Akka* workshops.

For some members of the textile designer profession, international exhibitions became the forum where they could present the results of their work and receive due response. The Finnish public and decision-makers were not interested in the past, nor did they always understand things new. Time, strength and resolute faith were need for the new to mature. The textile designer's work began to resemble the visual arts, just as solitary and financially insecure, but also independent and lacking restrictions laid down by others. In spite of this, countless crafts schools, adult education institutes, summer courses and hobby circles fanned interest in the field. Aesthetic content and technical standards were outweighed by craftsmanship.

In 1976 the first Nordic touring triennial of textile design was on show in Turku. Major international exhibitions of textile design in Lausanne, Switzerland and Lodz, Poland broadened the concept of textile design, lending support to the skills and expertise that had been doubted in Finland. During the first twenty years of the Lausanne exhibitions, Lea Tennberg, Sirpa Yarmolinsky, Kirsti Rantanen and Irma Kukkasjärvi were among the few designers accepted to exhibit their works. Textile design came off the walls and looms, boldly adopting and applying new combinations of materials. The pieces could grow ten-fold in size, or shrink to microscopic proportions.

On an equal footing

The international recognition of Finnish textile design, its renewal and the designers' persistence and faith in their own efforts began to bear fruit. In 1977–80 when Parliament House in Helsinki came under renovation, textile design was prominently involved. In addition to the interior textiles, Irma Kukkasjärvi also designed a three-part ryijy relief for the reception area for foreign delegations (1982). The large wall-hung piece commissioned from Maija Lavonen for the Speaker's office was completed in 1983. A year previously Lavonen had been given a 15-year state artist grant. In 1983 Kirsti Rantanen was awarded the title of Honorary Arts Professor and in 1984 she became the first representative of the design sector in the State Art Works Committee. Fewer jobs were available in industry, but commissions for textile works in public buildings, solo and

◀ *The printed fabric* Unikko *(Poppy) startled people with its big and bold figures. It was designed by Maija Isola for Marimekko in 1965. After thirty years, it is still in production and just as popular.*

Irma Kukkasjärvi

▲ *When the Parliament of Finland was renovated Irma Kukkasjärvi designed a three part ryijy relief for the Reception room in 1982. It is familiar for most Finns, as many interviews for TV have been filmed with the ryijy as background*

▶▶ *Maija Lavonen,* Haukivesi, *1985, a textile work with several parts, linen and silk, 650 x 220 x 550 cm. The city library of Varkaus, music department.*

▶ *The winner of the competition for a work of art for the Helsinki Opera House was Kirsti Rantanen in 1993 with* Sävelkudos *(Note Weave) a textile work constructed of colourful rope-like spirals and consisting of two parts which brings to mind a sculpture. It hangs on opposite walls of the foyer of the Opera.*

The Finnish National Opera/Matti Peltonen

group exhibitions and competitions increased in number. In 1980, after an interval of 35 years, the Evangelical-Lutheran Congregations of Helsinki held a design competition for ecclesiastical textiles and in 1981 TEXO began to elect the Textile Designer of the Year to promote recognition of the work of its members. In 1999, this title went to Outi Tuominen-Mäkinen, a recognized designer of printed interior textiles and garment fabrics. Tuominen-Mäkinen notes that her own textile pieces and her teaching and instruction works are a necessary counterweight to work with manufacturers and firms.

An important indication of the recognized and equal standing of textile design alongside other visual arts was the competition for invited entrants held for a work of textile art for Helsinki's new Opera House. The winner was Kirsti Rantanen with *Sävelkudos* (Note Weave). Consisting of two parts, fiery red Carmen and coolly blue Juha, it does not represent any traditional textile technique. The piece is constructed of colourful rope-like spirals, intertwined and layered to form an airy pillar. It seeks to operate freely as a composition of independent elements leaving the surrounding architectonic space unbroken.

Simo Rista

Finlayson

Outi Tuominen-Mäkinen, Ystävät *(Friends), printed fabric, Finlayson Barker Design, 1998. This design received a prize at an international textile competition held in Kyoto, Japan in 1997.*

Ecclesiastical and academic textile design

Research in textile design is a a new phenomenon of the 1990s. It has even given rise to doctoral dissertations. In 1991 Joint research projects involving the Department of Textile Design at the University of Art and Design Helsinki and the Department of Art History and teacher training at the University of Helsinki have resulted in studies of varying scope from brief research papers to graduate-school work.

◀ Lähde *(The Spring), a linen fabric designed by Fujiwo Ishimoto for Marimekko's autumn 1999 collection. The glasses on the table are designed by Brita Flander.*

From metal to plastics

Contemporary textile design is rich and varied, just like the works of the nuns of Naantali five hundred years ago. Today's materials and the shape, size and execution of textile design are limited only by the designer's imagination. The whole definition of textiles has become much broader, especially with materials such as metal, paper, fibreglass or plastics now in use. Definitions and boundaries as such are not important; the total aesthetic and visual effect of the pieces carries more weight. A work of textile art has fulfilled one of its functions when it has touched the heart and mind of its viewer.

A Story of Modern Finnish Furniture

Anne Stenros

▶ *The* Moduli *chest of drawers was designed by Pirkko Stenros in 1955 for the Muurame furniture company and is still being produced. It is part of a modular storage furniture system.*

▼ *The Vaara brothers furniture factory, 1924*

Unique and Universal

Modern Finnish furniture emerged from the serial manufacture of bent-wood furniture designed by Alvar Aalto. Their streamlined, minimalist lines have been one of the basic starting points of the modern Finnish furniture industry from the 1930s to the present day. These, too, have specific examples and prototypes: the tubular furniture of modernism on the one hand, and traditional, simple vernacular chairs and tables on the other hand. More importantly, however, Aalto furniture (chairs and tables) marked the beginning of a period of furniture as individual objects of applied arts, and later design products. Previously, items of furniture had been either ordinary utility objects or part of a designed interior and architectural entity in the applied arts sense. In this connection, they were usually made for individual and unique use. Aalto's furniture became serially manufactured products of applied arts for modern habitation and general use.

Pst-Moduli

Around the end of the 19th century, Finland's cabinet-making industry was in a marked period of change and growth. The Nikolai Boman furniture factory was one of the largest in the country, making products for both the domestic market and export. At the turn of the century, the furniture industry relied on commissions, and only simple, low-cost, utility furniture was made in series.

New aesthetic concepts and objectives appeared in the cabinet-making and furniture-manufacturing tradition around the turn of the 19th and 20th centuries. The first furniture shops and salesrooms were established in the early 1900s. One of the most important firms was the Iris company, founded by Count Louis Sparre. Iris based its products on national motifs and materials in the spirit of the international Arts and Crafts movement, and it was the first company to produce furniture in small series instead of individually crafted pieces. The products were presented to the public as complete interior designs including textiles and lamps.

Also around the turn of the 19th and 20th centuries, the young architects Herman Gesellius, Armas Lindgren and Eliel Saarinen designed and built the Hvitträsk studio and villa as an aesthetic entity, in which the individual items of furniture had the role of works of art complementing the architectural design as a whole. The interior was an integral part of the architecture and the furniture was created upon its conditions.

Nursery furniture, tables, chairs, textiles and other items were designed for Hvitträsk. The interior design was a unique creation. Many other contemporary artists' homes, such as Kalela at Ruovesi and Halosenniemi in Tuusula, were given a special interior as part of the overall architectural design.

Alvar Aalto's furniture was often created in connection with architectural projects as a solution to specific problems. The Paimio chair was originally designed for

Museum of Finnish Architecture

The Viipuri Library and its auditorium, designed by Alvar Aalto in 1930–35. The famous three-legged stool, which is still in production, was designed by Aalto in 1932.

► *Artek chair* 68, *originally designed by Alvar Aalto for the Viipuri Library in 1933–35. Chair 68 is still in production.*

the Paimio sanatorium, and the all-purpose chair *68* was made for the Viipuri City Library. The designs were later sold by Artek in Helsinki as serially produced items. Many Aalto lamps were also designed to complement the architecture of specific buildings, and were taken into production as basic models only at a later stage.

Göran Schildt has commented on Aalto's interior-design elements in the following terms:

"His interest in these 'architectural accessories' did not arise from any ambition to create a Gesamtkunstwerk, combining different art forms to produce an exclusive, aesthetic symphony: Aalto was motivated by the desire to offer people practical and functional buildings and everyday objects that were simultaneously symbols of a special philosophy of life, derived from nature and tinged with humanism."

These two basic factors of being attuned to nature and the practical combined with the idea of a total interior design have been important points of departure for modern Finnish furniture. The aspect of nature generally implies the use of domestic timber, and the practical approach has been associated with an emphasis on the function of furniture and their adaptability.

Since the 1920s, the furniture industry has concentrated in and around the city of Lahti in South Finland. Among other companies, the Mikko Nupponen factory and Lahden Puusepäntehdas, founded by August Avonius, and later renamed Asko-Avonius Oy and Asko Oy, moved to Lahti. Many recognized designers, such as Arttu Brummer and Ilmari Tapiovaara designed furniture for the Asko factories in the 1930s. The streamlined designs of Werner West and Arttu Brummer preceded Asko's furniture classics. Around this time, P. E. Blomstedt designed modern tubular furniture.

The evolution of furniture and lamps from utility objects and elements of interior decoration into products of applied arts, with an intrinsic value regardless of the overall interior design, was particularly underlined in the 1950s. Design and the applied arts were viewed from the perspective of individual objects, often unique pieces, at numerous exhibitions and similar events, such as the Milan Triennials. More and more furniture was now initially designed for serial manufacture without any connection with or origin in an architectonic whole, building or interior design scheme.

Ilmari Tapiovaara was one of the forerunners of the functional and rational approach. Many of his furniture designs were modern and international before their time. Production figures for his *Domus* and *Nana* chairs exceeded the one-million mark and they were exported to many countries in Europe and to the United States. Serial manufacture and export were characteristic of the Finnish furniture industry of the 1950s and 1960s. Tapiovaara's objective was to develop a so-called all-purpose chair that could be adapted to as many uses as possible. The former consideration of an individual use-related situation was now replaced

Artek

Museum of Art and Design/Rauno Träskelin

The Domus *chair, designed by Ilmari Tapiovaara in 1946, was made of bent plywood. It was originally designed for the Domus Academica student housing facility in Helsinki. The production of the chair has been resumed.*

by the need to find a general and universal solution to the needs of dwelling and habitation in the post-war era.

The concept of adaptability and the modern lifestyle, inherent, for instance, in the design philosophy of Kaj Franck, was also adopted in furniture design. The former large, rigid and space-consuming suites of furniture were now being replaced by the manufacture of easily convertible, individually assembled and flexible elements of interior design.

New collections of furniture, such as children's furniture and modular storage units designed by Pirkko Stenros for the Muurame company carried on the tradition of furniture based on interior design. The same items could be used for various interiors, from bedrooms to living rooms. These items of furniture reflected the idea of a lifestyle and interior design as the starting point for designing furniture, as opposed to "unique" items of furniture isolated from their setting. Following the spirit of modernism, their purpose was a general function with individual variations.

Since the 1960s, Finnish furniture and its design have clearly reflected two different starting points and approaches. On the one hand there was furniture designed as elements of interior design, and on the other hand there were individual items of design furniture. Good examples of the latter concept are plastic chairs designed by Eero Aarnio in the 1960s, such as *Pallo* (Ball), which was a purely object-derived item of furniture, whose independent role in interior design was particularly underlined. Also Yrjö Kukkapuro's plastic chairs of the 1960s, such as *Karuselli* (Carousel) were design products that dominated their space.

Object-based furniture is characterized by a susceptibility to trends; they are closely attuned to the spirit of the times and some of them can later develop into classics. Yrjö Kukkapuro for instance varied his chair designs in keeping with the spirit of the times. In the 1960s his furniture borrowed themes from pop art; the 1970s saw a focus on ergonomics; in the 1980s Kukkapuro was a pioneer of postmodernism in Finland; and in the 1990s his works have exhibited a minimalist spirit.

Another example of creating individual design products is the furniture of Antti Nurmesniemi, whose *Triennial chair*, presented in prototype form at Milan in the 1960s, did not come into production until the late 1990s. Reduced, streamlined lines or figures are characteristic of Nurmesniemi's works. This is most clearly evident in a "graphic" single-line armchair designed by him in the 1970s.

Pst-Moduli/PF-Studio, Pietinen

The Pallo (Ball) chair by Eero Aarnio, 1963. This chair constitutes a space within a space. Its production was resumed in the late 1990s.

▲ *Nursery and children's furniture designed by Pirkko Stenros for Muurame in the 1960s. The objective was to create flexible ensembles for the interior design of the home.*

The streamlined fibreglass Karuselli *(Carousel) chair was designed by Yrjö Kukkapuro in 1965. It is in the collections of many museums around the world and is currently made by Avarte.*

Museum of Art and Design/PF-Studio, Pietinen

Museum of Art and Design/Manne Stenros

Piiroinen

Vivero

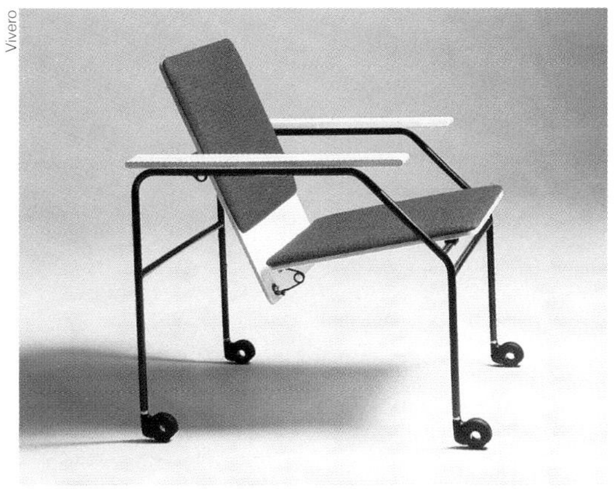

Martela

◀ *The* Kari 3 *chair, designed by Kari Asikainen for the P. O. Korhonen company, received the SIO Interior Architects Association award in 1982.*

◀◀ *The* Visio 100 *chair by Simo Heikkilä and Yrjö Wiherheimo, 1980. The spring between the seat and the backrest provides comfort in use.*

Artek

Ben af Schultén designed chair 414 *for Artek in 1979. The chair marked a contemporary addition to the Artek range of furniture.*

Natural and National

The next generation of designers of modern furniture began their professional careers in the late 1970s, during the years of the energy crisis. Plastics and metal went out of use and domestic wood again came to the fore.

Simo Heikkilä and Yrjö Wiherheimo were pioneers of their generation. Among other works, they designed wooden and metal furniture of a new and structurally light appearance for the Vivero company, to be used in public spaces and offices. Throughout the 1980s and '90s Simo Heikkilä continued his series of experimental wooden chairs, seeking to minimize the use of material in the individual product while promoting the use of domestic species of timber and the Finnish tradition of cabinetmaking. Heikkilä's experiments of the late 1990s include the use of birch bark in furniture.

Ben af Schultén added to Artek's line of furniture by designing classical chairs, sofas and tables. Chair *414*, created in the 1980s, is one of the best known of these works. During the 1980s Kari Asikainen designed a large number of chairs for the P.O. Korhonen company. Of these, the bent-wood all-purpose chair *Kari 3* was one of the most successful products.

Domestic materials, mainly birch and birch veneer, were characteristic of furniture design throughout the early 1980s in Finland. Despite this natural and national starting point, the result was a definitely contemporary and original image, which at best was able to compete on an even footing with international trends and manufacturers. Many presentations of furniture at fairs, for example in Milan and Cologne in the 1980s, received a great deal of publicity and acclaim. The fresh, light Nordic image accentuated with colourful textiles

◀ *The* Triennaali-tuoli *(Triennial chair) with its graphic lines was designed by Antti Nurmesniemi for the Milan Triennials of 1960. It did not reach the production stage until 1997, when the Piiroinen company began to make it .*

Rintala Meuble

Design Forum Finland/Sameli Rantanen

Workshop of Rintala Meuble, a family-owned company.

in a contemporary spirit found a great deal of praise – as well as many buyers and users. Large quantities of Finnish furniture were exported in the 1980s.

The continuity of Northern modernism and the use of Finnish wood have also been furthered and upheld in the 1990s by Jouko Järvisalo and Tuula Falk. Järvisalo's prize-winning chairs and his new, light structures in wood are extremely minimalist designs, with the *Kova A* chair and its different versions as one example.

Designing for Rintala Meuble, Tuula Falk has created a number of more traditional cupboards and chairs, in which high-class craftsmanship is as prominent a factor as form. The revival of the cabinetmaking tradition in the 1990s is also present in Falk's designs, for example her *Sonetti* cupboard. Markku Kosonen and Kari Virtanen are important figures in the cabinetmaking tradition and proponents of Finnish wood. The 1990s has also witnessed a partial return to the handcrafted manufacture of furniture in small series, especially in solid-wood furniture.

National starting points, natural materials and simple, practical form constitute the core line underscored in the wooden furniture of the 1980s and particularly in their successors in the 1990s.

◄ Rintala Meuble produces the Sonetti *cupboard by Tuula Falk. The cupboard is part of the Sonetti collection designed by Falk in the 1990s.*

Kari Virtanen

Cabinetmaker Kari Virtanen has a workshop at Fiskars. All the furniture is made of solid wood and with wood joints.

The Experiment *chair designed by Yrjö Kukkapuro in 1982–83 for Avarte. This chair heralded the advent of postmodern design in Finland.*

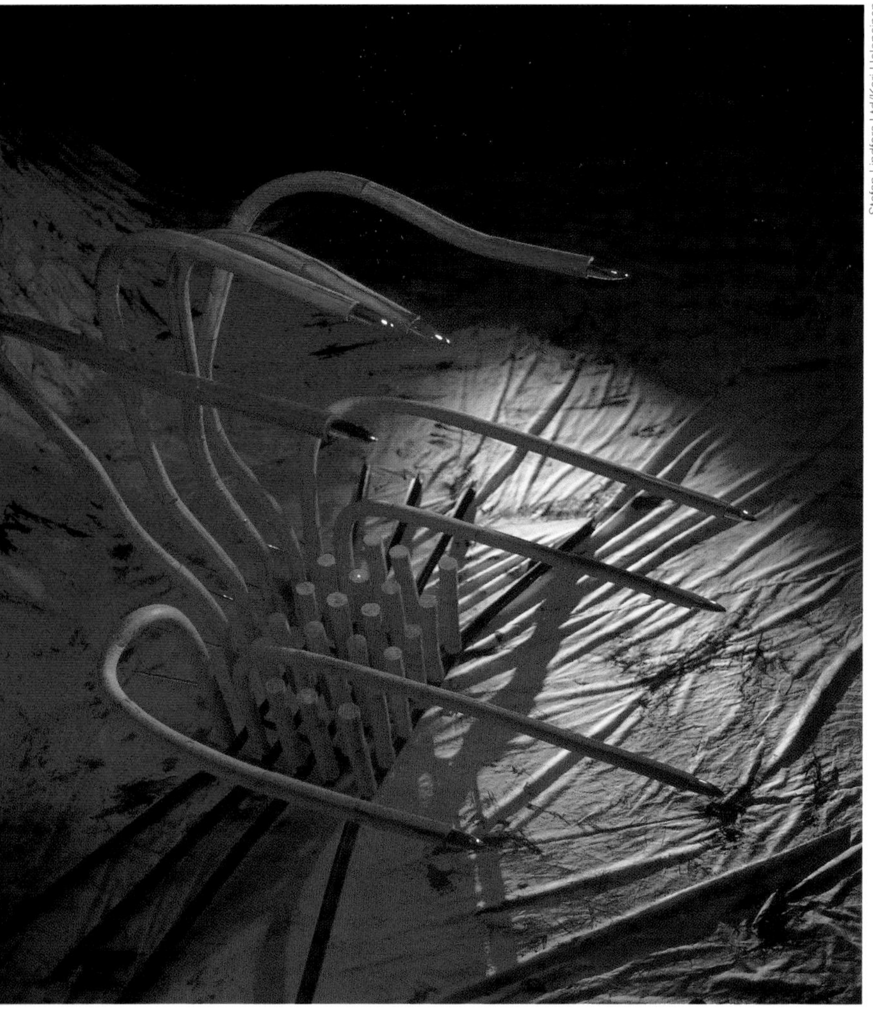

Stefan Lindfors Ltd/Kari Holopainen

In 1987, Stefan Lindfors designed a number of sculptural thrones for the Metaxis exhibition, featuring young designers. Shown here is The Scorpion *(160 x 90 x 200 cm).*

Experimental and International

A new era of individuality began in design in the mid-1980s. The postmodernism in design that stemmed from the Italian furniture industry introduced experimentation, a search for things new and a new image of colour and form also into Finnish furniture.

Yrjö Kukkapuro's colourful experiments in design with his Experiment chairs were the first manifestations of the new wave in Finland. Stefan Lindfors's chair installations for the Metaxis exhibition of the late 1980s were also Finland's introduction to the completely new idea of conceptual design in furniture.

In the late 1980s furniture for public space in particular, such as office furniture, experienced a new boom with the construction and interior decoration of many new public buildings, cultural centres, city halls and company head offices. Martela Oy and Vivero Oy, among other companies, developed new office furniture. Towards the end of the decade international trends superseded explicitly national starting points. Now, the materials, colours and themes reflected a new, multi-faceted era.

There has been a wide range of materials, form, colour and techniques throughout the 1990s. Experimental and conceptual furniture, presented by young designers as prototypes or as self-produced small series, have received wide and significant attention especially in the international press. Finnish furniture was "rediscovered" after the recession and slow years of the early 1990s.

Stefan Lindfors's experiments with materials and form in objects and in the visual arts have set an example for many young designers beginning their careers. An independent and autonomous freelance designer collaborating with many manufacturers has come to replace the former long-term relationships between designers and companies. The young furniture designers of today are networked and have even begun to produce and market their products.

The Snowcrash group, founded in 1997 and Timo Salli and Ilkka Suppanen of its members, as well as Pasi Pänkäläinen, Sari Anttonen and Harri Koskinen represent a completely new conception of Finnish furniture and the way of life in the late 1990s. Finnishness or national starting points are no longer at issue, but rather a networked society and globalization dominated by the information society, cosmopolitan, nomad and urban are among the terms used to describe the views jointly held by the young designers and their products.

Martela

◀ *The late 1980s marked the beginning of a period of furniture for public space and offices. The Amfi office furniture collection was made by Martela in the 1980s.*

▼ The Tangent *workstation produced by Martela in the 1990s and designed by Pekka Toivola and the Martela product development team.*

Martela

The rapid expansion of information technology, the resulting changes in society, the new European Finland, and the marked growth and globalization of the market economy are all reflected in the way in which young designers create, produce and market their furniture. The product concept in particular has been characteristic of furniture of the late 1990s.

The era of serially manufactured utility furniture and interior design elements has given way to experimental individual items of furniture or marketing-oriented small series of products. The former individuality of unique interior designs has now been replaced by individuality in an experimental, conceptual and even abstract sense. Items of furniture have become separate design objects, with no links to time, place or setting. A good example of this trend is provided by the product imagery of contemporary furniture, unrelated to any context or place and appearing to "float" in the air. The objective here is a product as universal, global and "pure" as possible.

During the 1950s and '60s Finnish furniture was presented in the exhibition environment of the Milan Triennials. In the 1970s and '80s trade fairs placed Finnish furniture on the international scene, and now in the 1990s, particularly at its close, Finnish design products are being presented through the international design media.

A number of young Finnish designers have found their way into the international market and to collaborate with foreign manufacturers. For instance, Cappellini of Italy produces Ilkka Suppanen's *Flying Carpet* divan and a Swedish investment company recently bought the Snowcrash brand and range of products.

The future will show how the public will discover and accept the new, independent, mobile and global lifestyle inherent in the furniture of young designers.

The tale of modern design furniture in Finland is a narrative of the everyday. The starting point is changing everyday life and its specific conditions – both restrictions and opportunities. Added to this point of departure was an aesthetic reflecting not only national features but also contemporary international goals and ideals. Many of the successful results of this process have become everyday classics – from one generation to another.

Avarte

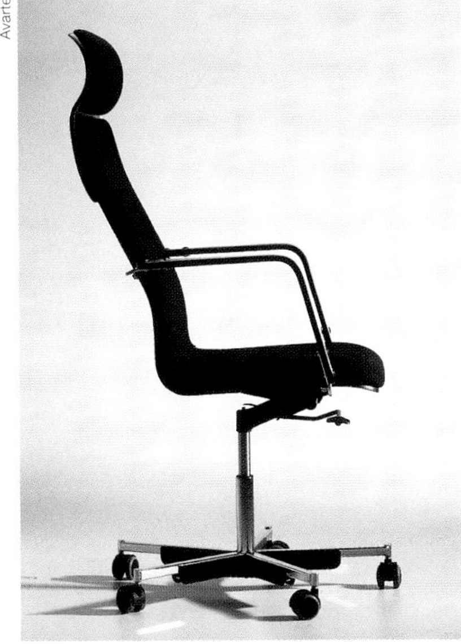

◀ *Yrjö Kukkapuro's* Fysio *chair from the 1980s carried on his series of ergonomic chairs for the workplace.*

▼ *Jouni Leino's* Net *computer desk and chair from 1999 were originally designed for the renovation project of the Helsinki School of Economics and Business Administration.*

Avarte

Vivero

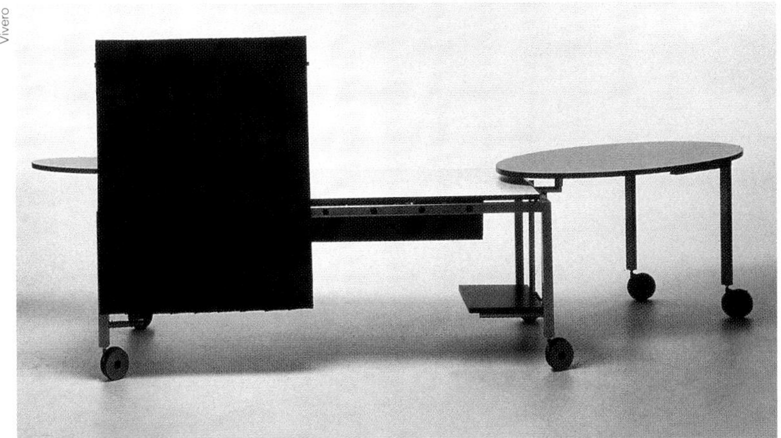

Vivero's Plus *office furniture collection from the late 1990s, designed by Yrjö Wiherheimo and Pekka Kojo. The Vivero company has been a forerunner of the flexible and adaptable office concept in Finland.*

Periferia Design/Rauno Träskelin

Simo Heikkilä's Tumppi *chair for watching television represents a completely new kind of design. Prototype from 1999.*

Artek

Ben af Schultén designed the Espa *chair for Artek in 1999.*

▶ *The* Kova A *chair, designed by Jouko Järvisalo and made by the Mobel company, received the main prize in the Pro Finnish Design awards in 1999.*

The Brand is the Signature of Design

Pekka Toivanen

To a great degree, design has become a service profession. This long-standing objective among designers has now been largely realized. The subjective bricoleur, sculptor and artist have given way to the design consult, industrial designer and design expert. The development of the designer's professional profile has been fast and has concerned the idioms means and expectations of work in terms of results, as well as related attitudes.

In seeking to understand the ways in which the designer's profession has developed and its future description we must pause to review this complete renewal of means and concepts in the working environment of the industrial designer. At present, the professional image of the industrial designer is so closely associated with technology and electronics that we may well ask how industrial design at all can be incorporated into the tradition and concept of the applied arts.

We should point out here that the image of Finnish design was created with design products aestheticized by artist-designers, and by offering the rest of the world Northern uniqueness, mysticism and personality. Art and industry found each other specifically in design and references explaining Finnish design were sought in the visual arts, literature, folk poetry and music. Creativity, especially the Northern sensuality of colour and aesthetic sense, were readily seen as resulting almost directly from the Finns' relationship with nature and the wilderness. In this story, half of which was true and half of which was an excellently scripted and directed marketing of an image of Finland, design was almost art. Ultimately, the actual product was not a photogenic design object but in fact a photograph of it, replicated as a feast for the eyes in read and browsed interior design and fashion magazines, all the way to far-off America. This created the image that made it possible to market more mundane objects, even utility ware for the dining table.

But what is the role of design in a community of nation-states, where mass production is based on developed technology and where national uniqueness is almost outmoded and old-fashioned. This question has been timely wherever production has become mechanized, industrialized and international. The significance of design in applying technology has become underscored, because the complex technology of manufacture begins to be mundane and available to all manufacturers. Machinery and purely technical solutions in products and the organization of production are no longer a sufficient competitive advantage in the market.

Industrial design today wants to be integrated as part of Finnish competitiveness. Design is seen as providing opportunities with which also Finnish industry can be successful in international competition. There are grounds to claim that as late as thirty years ago Finnish design promoted and marketed Finnish culture and our national identity. The designer represented the nation abroad in the same way as a long-distance runner or a composer. But now design represents the know-how that can add to the skills of a company the means to take it further and faster ahead than its competitors.

In speaking of the global market we must bear in mind that manufacturing has also gone global. Nationality is not the main concern for the identity and strategy of successful companies, but rather the assured precondition for international competitiveness and operations. The electronics industry is an extreme example of how competition forces companies to relocate production in countries providing low-cost labour. As a result, the industrial infrastructure is dispersed throughout the world, and clusters of high technology can be found just as well in a poor Chinese rural commune as in an affluent EU member state.

As technology takes on an everyday character the importance of design work is emphasized. This takes place because creative skills cannot be replicated or produced artificially. It is possible to plagiarize or imitate the manufacturing systems, brand names and products of designers, but the creative capital of another company cannot be borrowed. Design has become one the most important competitive assets for companies for the reason that design proficiency can-

▶ Fiskars Clippers *gardening tool, Olavi Lindén, 1997, Fiskars Consumer Oyj. The series of pruners and clippers has won a number of international design awards.*

FISKARS
FISKARS
FISKARS
STAINLESS FINLAND
FISKARS
STAINLESS FINLAND
FISKARS
STAINLESS FINLAND

Fiskars

Handy *axes, Olavi Lindén, Svante Rönnholm, Timo Sunila, Kenneth Wickström/Fiskars, 1992, Fiskars Consumer Oyj*

▶ *Valmet OptiConcept papermaking line, Risto Väätänen and Petteri Venetjoki/Valmet, 3d Muotoilutoimisto, ARCH Design and the Valmet product development team, 1996–98, Valmet Corporation.*

■ *Valmet's director of design, Risto Väätänen, was chosen as the Industrial Designer of the Year 1999. He is in charge of designing Valmet's product development of paper machines. The picture shows part of the team: Markku Järvensivu, Petteri Venetjoki and Risto Väätänen.*

Fiskars

The original Fiskars multipurpose scissors, Olof Backström, 1960s, Fiskars Consumer Oyj.

not be stolen. This identity is created within a company from the attitudes, skills and activities of its employees. It is with the aid of design that the company's own identity is given visible expression, a tangible form.

Along with innovations in production technology and the developed market, the designer's job description has become more diverse. Alongside the problem solving of traditional design, such as selection of materials, ergonomics, applications for manufacture and artefact-related aesthetics, there have appeared completely new long-term strategic objectives, in turn related to facilitating corporate communications and company image with the aid of design. Design quality, the overall appearance of objects and services, has become an indicator revealing a company's potential and know-how. Individual design objects no longer suffice to create a sustainable positive image even for traditional design companies; credibility arises from results evident as renewing design and design strategy.

Design strategy is not only important in product design and for the consumer. Design by a company enhances the degree to which products and services are processed and refined, thus having an effect on the value of the company as a whole. The level of design proficiency is an important factor in assessing the financial value of a company, for example from the investor's perspective. The history of brands often involves a successful long-term design programme, with which a company has been able to distinguish itself into the area beyond the ordinary and the mediocre.

In the 21st century this area will still be the dimension of the product world in which the product will entail a promise of better overall quality. It is a promise of a product being more than its physical and technological structure. In products of this kind, the mark of creativity and skill remains even after mass production. The consumer may value a brand as much as an artist's signature.

In particular, consumer goods containing new technology undergo constant product development, because new technological solutions renew the range of products increasingly faster and more and more often. In this course of development, design has had to adapt to the cycle dictating technological innovation. At the same time design has emphasized a closer human approach to balance the technological aspect. More than ever before, the claim is proven that it is the designer who is on the side of the consumer in product development.

The technology-boundedness of industrial design has also spelt the adoption of a completely new kind of thinking in design. Speed is important, and often even decisive. Therefore a design office must be able to offer its client companies an efficient design process. There is an emphasis on goal-orientation and accountability. In practice, advanced data processing has made it possible to raise potential. During the 1990s, Finnish design offices and design education have replaced drawing boards with computers and simulation programs. The designer's opportunities to present new ideas for products and visions for the future have undergone a revolution. Previously, one of the most time-consuming stages of the design process was to prepare presentation images and the visual presentation of new product ideas. Now computer-assisted simulation makes it possible to create products in virtual reality. The information and data necessary for making them can be transferred directly from the computer files of

Yrjö Tuunanen
Valmet

the design office to the manufacturer. Also manufacturing technology and the organization of production can be simulated with computers in the design stage. Computer technology is a virtual short cut to the future that is continually used by designers in product development.

State-of-the-art object simulators can create a disturbing artificially real impression of objects and space. The virtual dimension created by computer displays and simulation programs cannot, however, provide a sensation comparable to real touch, taste, smell, sight and hearing. Therefore, the path of design still includes the making of models and prototypes. The designer gives concrete form to product ideas, artefactualizing information and implementing a practical design strategy. Despite continuously developing data-technological aids the work of a designer concentrating on objects always includes practical aspects.

The purpose of applying data technology in design is not to replace existing reality with a virtual world but to make it possible to review and compare alternative ideas from the very beginning of the product-design process. Virtual reality is no substitute for the designer's own observations and the 3D programs of computers cannot replace the ability to see and draw sketches and studies, even though they are an efficient means for presenting and recording ideas. The final approval of a product and its practicality can only be established in trial use and tests.

Interestingly, many of the most skilled craftsmen have found an opportunity to work in industrial product design. The making of models and prototypes has become a special crafts occupation associated with design, especially when the developing professional identity of industrial designers more readily dresses them in the uniform of a business suit than in overalls. The makers of prototypes often have so-called artisan level vocational training and have found themselves a core role in product design through their own skills. They could be compared to the master mould-makers of the glass industry, who still work in immediate contact with the designer. The particular fascination of modelling lies in its combination of traditional pride in craftsmanship with contemporary manufacturing technology. Craftsmanship and crafts skills are often regarded as the opposite of industrial mass production. The making of models and prototypes, however, is one of the cornerstones of implementing industrial design, upon which the whole credibility of the design process is based. A computer-assisted virtual-reality presentation cannot compete with the impression of a few actual prototypes of the new product. The model-maker creates unique pieces. Along with traditional tools, he or she works more and more with computer-assisted means that can utilize the 3D model made by the designer. The most common of these is the CNC cutter with which it is relatively easy to make prototypes or their parts to be assembled into a functioning prototype. In making prototypes industrial designers are increasingly using technical rapid modelling means, 3D office printers and so-called "rapid tooling" equipment. These are new rapid manufacturing techniques making it possible to create a facsimile model, a prototype, or even a tool for experimental manufacture.

The most important progress experienced in design is not, however, related to the designer's means and tools. Design proficiency has also found new content as a result of the fact that companies want to utilize the designer's efforts efficiently. In drawing up briefs and designing products there is now focus on producing analyses and information that will improve the designer's opportunities to solve problems. Marketing-based expertise on consumers and competition has a growing influence on the content of the briefs assigned by designers. New models have also been developed in the design process for considering the wishes of consumers. Usability studies have become part of the design path. Especially because of electronics, usability has become an important factor influencing design, for it is integrally associated with the problems and considerations of every electronics-based product. Design has achieved a key role in the artefactualization of the technology contained in devices. A good mobile phone is naturally the fruit of co-operation involving many experts. Electronics design, programming, research into materials, product logistics, and, for example, marketing, are all core factors in successful product design. But in the final analysis, it is design that gives even electronics a functioning and user-friendly texture and physical dimensions.

User interfaces are evolving into a completely separate category of design. Growing numbers of graduate projects in industrial design concern man's relationship with machinery and equipment and the ability to communicate with them. Computer's, digital television, the Internet, mobile communications devices and the automation met by consumers in everyday life have created a completely new need to facilitate man–machine communication. A whole new generation has emerged as advanced technology has become an everyday matter. This generation has a straightforward and inquisitive attitude to rapidly renewing technological products. The lifestyles and consumer behaviour of young people have created a new and dynamically developing market also for design. In order to expand and maintain an achieved share of the market, companies must undertake continuous efforts and ever-faster product development. It has become obvious

Timberjack

Walking harvester, prototype, 1995, Timberjack Oy. Kone is testing the applicability of walking technology to forest work.

Tractors and harvesters

Tractors and harvesters are an integral part of the rural landscape of Finland. Tractors are multi-functional machines and mechanical power units that have achieved a high degree of sophistication in terms of output and ergonomics. The farmer no longer has to sit in the open in the dust; the tractor cabin is a comfortable and safe working environment.

Valmet

▲ *Diesel tractor, 1961, Jukka Pellinen, the Tourula plant of Valmet Oy.*

E&D Design

▶ *Tractor cabin, E&D Design, 1996, Valmet Corporation*

The harvester can be described as an offspring of the tractor for forest use. Contemporary harvester design is focusing more and more on the impact of the machine itself on the forest environment. Today's lumberjack has given up the power saw for a forest harvester cabin installed with data technology, for felling and cutting with the aid of a joystick. Many versions of this multi-purpose forestry machine have been developed with the aid of design and engineering. The most recent one literally walks to the logging site.

Tractors and harvesters are developed and made by industrial designers and the engineering industry for hard work and arctic conditions. One of the main considerations of Finnish industrial design is to help people work better in environments of long distances and harsh conditions.

that work in design will continuously become more challenging and difficult.

The requirement today is to create growing numbers of product entities that have a strong identity and are environmentally conscious. The challenges presented by industry to designers are so varied and significant that, from an increasingly earlier stage, the designers of the future will have to specialize, for example, in usability, user interfaces, electronics products, means of transport or design strategy. The environmental effects of industry have also posed new, and welcome, objectives for design. Life-span analyses of products are considerations no less important to product design than usability or adaptation to manufacture. The charting of the environmental effects of a product idea will become more and more important when considering the conditions for manufacturing a new product.

In addition to product design and design strategy on the part of companies, the opportunities of society to apply design expertise are diversified by design research carried out in the universities and polytechnics. Non-commercial research injects new content into the debate on the values of design, which will also help in steering design in firms and companies. Design research will increase conceptual means to comprehend design, the opportunities it entails, and the nature of design as a profession. Design education has also been made available to students in technical and commercial fields, by which it has been sought to promote cooperation between designers and other professional groups involved in the design process. The results of these efforts in shaping attitudes can be seen in working life. Design is no longer something left to designers alone; the implementation of design strategy is being increasingly monitored at the executive level.

Changes in the status of design and designers, and their role in society, have only begun. Young as a profession, industrial design has distanced itself from its actual starting points in arts and crafts and has sought to complement in a new way the ability of industry to control and apply technological progress. The designer is accepted among the experts applying new technology and creating products from it. The tasks of design extend from the shaping of products to planning and designing corporate communications, brands and design strategies. The traditional "studio" of a company has become a design department creating visions and peering into the future, with the responsibility of keeping design as one of the company's competitive assets. The attitudes and professional skills of the new generation of designers will largely dictate how design will be able to maintain the significant role in industry and society that it is finally achieving.

Creadesign/Rauno Träskelin

The Helsinki metro and trams

Public transport is a continuous source of challenges for industrial design. The Helsinki metro is a subject of discussion and debate at the turn of the millennium, and there are plans to extend the present line to Espoo, situated to the west of Helsinki. In use since 1982, the Helsinki metro is a prime example of successful design outliving changing styles and trends. Its orange colour has become a symbol of rapid, comfortable urban transport. Originally the largest industrial design project of its day, the Helsinki metro carriages were designed by Börje Rajalin and Antti Nurmesniemi.

Cities with a functioning tram system provide their inhabitants with a convenient means of public transport. An element of change and renewal in the urban environment, Helsinki's new tram model received an honorary mention in the Pro Finnish Design competition of 1999. Olavi Hänninen was originally one of the designers of Helsinki's standard tram model, introduced in the 1970s. The new model rolled onto the streets during the summer of 1999. The new tram is an international product that has been adapted to the climate and terrain of Helsinki. The city's hilly and winding net-

Low-floor tram for Helsinki, Creadesign/Hannu Kähönen, 1996-98, Adtranz and Adtranz Finland.

work of tram lines led to changes in the construction of the tram, originally designed for German cities. These were not just external or cosmetic alterations. The new tram is better lit, more comfortable and warmer in winter weather, and it marks a radical improvement in driver ergonomics. The dimensions of the cab can be adjusted to the individual measurements of the drivers. The new tram was given its special Helsinki image by industrial designer Hannu Kähönen.

Helsinki City Transport

Helsinki metro carriage, Antti Nurmesniemi and Börje Rajalin, 1970s, Helsinki City Transport.

Tunturi

E&D Design

▲ T8 *exercise bike, E & D Design/Heikki Kiiski, Jussi Juva and Jouni Teittinen, 1999, Tunturi. It has ergonomic qualities comparable to a racing bike plus broad-spectrum adjustability. Equipped with a graphic interface.*

Polar Electro

▶ *The Titanium-cased* Polar M71 Ti *heart rate monitor for fitness enthusiasts. Muotoilutoimisto Linja Oy, 1999, Polar Electro Oy.*

▶▶ *Suunto's* Vector *and* Vyper *were designed for extreme situations. The picture shows the* Vyper *diving watch/computer, Eljas Perheentupa and Jorma Jaakkola, 1999, Suunto Oy.*

Leisure

Now firmly established in the North American market, Tunturi has grown from a bicycle factory based in Turku into a diverse manufacturing and marketing firm for sports and personal exercise products. *Tunturi's* ergonomically designed exercise monitoring equipment has permitted it to maintain its position in the market. Design is one of the most important competitive factors for products that have to withstand extreme conditions and convince the consumer of their functionality.

The growing amount of leisure time has also created new needs in the market. Polar is another Finnish brand that has employed design to create an appealing image of well-functioning and reliable product. In addition to sports enthusiasts, Polar is also focusing on the sectors of the market that are developing as the population grows older. Growing numbers of people are interested in monitoring their own health. Polar's heart rate and fitness monitors provide new opportunities for independent exercise and for improving one's own performance. Tunturi and Polar have developed their own design strategy that will ensure of the range of products in time. Work in the sector of design is carried out by the companies' own industrial designers as well as by design offices, complementing the design expertise of the companies.

The wristwatch-shaped *Vector* compass is a small device whose design permits it to be used even in extreme outdoor conditions. It gives the user the coordinates of his or her position in addition to telling the time and giving data on the weather. For the wilderness hiker and trekker the *Vector* will ensure the proper sense of time and place even when one's own instincts are no longer reliable. The various functions of the *Vector* are in a wristwatch-type housing resistant to shock, moisture and other shocks. The *Vector* is a good example of a typical problem of electronic products: a large number of functions in a small space that may have to be used in difficult conditions. The *Vector* compass is more of a tool than a trendy compass – use is given priority in its design. Nevertheless, this product projects an efficient, strong yet fashionable image, down to its packaging.

SUUNTO
SUUNTO
19.3
19.8
MAX
SET SIM MEM
23
NO DEC TIME
MODE
18
°C
16
DIVE TIME
PLAN
TIME

Nokia

▲ *Mobira* Talkman 510, *late 1980s. Nokia Mobile Phones. One of the earliest mobile phones.*

▲ Nokia 8810, *1998, Nokia Mobile Phones. The first real wireless 'design' phone.*

Communications

One of the most famous images of Finnish communications is Akseli Gallen-Kallela's painting *Shepherd Boy from Paanajärvi*, in which a young boy is blowing into a birch-bark horn in a desolate wilderness setting. Very few of today's communications products have achieved the same iconic role in folklore as the birch-bark horn. New telecommunications products appear in such rapid cycles that they no longer have time to become obsolete, not to mention finding a place in collective memory.

A few products, however, have succeeded in becoming logged in popular memory because of their design and marketing. Visiting Finland in 1989, former Soviet leader Mikhail Gorbachev was amazed by Mobira's state-of-the-art mobile phone. This model, the world's first cellular phone, soon became a tool for hurried businessmen and a reflection of its user's status. Over the course of a decade, the heavy phone, both looking and weighing like a brick, has become a low-cost consumer item in everyday use, providing links with the networks of the world and containing many of the functions of notebook computers. The design of cellular phones is influenced not only by considerations of use and function but also by fashion. Immediately upon being introduced, Nokia's new small mobile phone resembling a piece of costume jewellery achieved great popularity also because of its progressive design.

▶ *Finnish design became internationally renowned in the 1950s and '60s in the traditional fields of industrial arts, ceramics, glass, furniture and textiles. The concept of design and industrial design only came into being in the 1960s. Since the 1980s, industrial design has grown exponentially. In the 1990s growth was boosted by the rapid growth and range of applications of state-of-the-art electronics and information technology.*
Pastilli chair by Eero Aarnio, late 1960s, and
Nokia 5110 *mobile phone, late 1990s*

NOKIA

Bibliography

National Culture and Public Authority

Aspelin, Eliel: *Suomalaisen taiteen historia pääpiirteissään*, Suomalaisen Kirjallisuuden Seura. Helsinki, 1891.

Hausen, Marika & Mikkola, Kirmo & Amberg, Anna-Lisa & Valto, Tytti: *Eliel Saarinen, Projects 1896–1923.* Museum of Finnish Architecture, Helsinki, 1990.

Wäre, Ritva: *How Nationalism was Expressed in Finnish Architecture at the Turn of the Last Century. Art and the National Dream.* Edited by Nicola Gordon Bowe. Irish Academic Press 1993, 169–180, Dublin, 1993.

Wäre, Ritva: *Kalela and Tarvaspää – The Wanderer's Homes, Akseli Gallen-Kallela.* The Finnish National Gallery Ateneum 1996, 112–123, Helsinki, 1996.

Wäre, Ritva: *Rakennettu suomalaisuus. Nationalismi viime vuosisadan vaihteen arkkitehtuurissa ja sitä koskevissa kirjoituksissa.* Suomen Muinaismuistoyhdistyksen Aikakauskirja 95. Helsinki, 1991.

Functionalism and the Aaltos

Heinonen, Raija-Liisa: *Funktionalismin läpimurto Suomessa* (The breakthrough of Finnish functionalism), 1986.

Keinänen, Timo: Eskimonaisen nahkahousut ravintola Savoyn pöydällä (The leather pants of an Eskimo woman on the table of the Savoy restaurant), *Arkkitehti* 8/1980.

Kruskopf, Erik: *Finnish design 1875–1975: 100 vuotta suomalaista taideteollisuutta/visuaalinen historia* (A hundred year of Finnish industrial design).Timo Sarpaneva & Erik Bruun. Otava, Keuruu, 1975.

Maunula, Leena: Taideteollisuuden funktionalismin synty (The emergence of functionalism in industrial design), in *Ars – Suomen taide* 5/1990.

Ólafsdottir, Ásdis: Le mobilier d'Alvar *Aalto*, 1998.

Göran Schildt: *The Decisive Years*, Rizzoli, Keuruu, 1986.

Pekka Suhonen: *Artek – alku, tausta, kehitys,* 1985.

Out into the World

Kalha, Harri: *Muotopuolen merenneidon pauloissa. Suomen taideteollisuuden kultakausi: mielikuvat, markkinointi, diskurssit* (Ensnared by a disfigured mermaid. The golden age of Finnish design). Doctoral dissertation. Published by the Historical Society of Finland and the Museum of Art and Design. Helsinki, 1997.

Nikula, Riitta: (ed.): Sankar*uus ja arki. Suomen 50-luvun miljöö. Heroism and the Everyday. Building Finland in the 1950:s.* Museum of Finnish Architecture. Helsinki 1994.

Stritzler Levine, Nina & Marianne Aav (eds.): *Finnish Modern Design.* Bard Graduate Center and Yale University Press, New York, 1998.

Modern Glass Design

Interviews

Kerttu Nurminen, Heikki Orvola, Liisa Räsänen, Markku Salo, Nanny Still, Timo Sarpenava, Oiva Toikka, Helena Tynell, Maaria Wirkkala

Thank you
Kaisa Koivisto, The Museum of Finnish Glass

Bibliography :

Helena Tynell. Design 1943–1993. Exposition catalogue of the Museum of Finnish Glas. Hämeenlinna, 1998.

Iittala à la Triennale de Milan. Exposition catalogue of the Iittala Glassmuseum, 1987.

Kaj Franck. Muotoilija, Formgivare, Designer. Museum of Industrial Design & Werner Söderström Osakeyhtiö. Porvoo-Helsinki-Juva, 1992.

Kaj Franck.Teema ja muunnelmia. (Theme and variations). Publication of the City of Heinola n 6. Lahti, 1997.

Kalha, Harri: *Muotopuolen merenneidon pauloissa.* (Ensnared by a disfigured mermaid. The golden age of Finnish design). Doctoral dissertation. Published by the Historical Society of Finland and the Museum of Industrial Design. Jyväskylä, 1997.

Kalin, Kaj: *Sarpaneva*. Keuruu, 1986.

Koivisto, Kaisa: *Finnish Modern Design: Utopian Ideals and Everyday Realities, 1930–1997.* Edited by Marianne Aav and Nina Stritzler-Levine. Published by the Bard Graduate Center for Studies in the Decorative Arts and Yale University Press, New Haven and London, 1998.

The Modern Spirit – Glass from Finland. Exposition

catalogue. Museum of Finnish Glass. Helsinki, 1985.

Moderne Zeiten. Finnisches Glas 1929–1999. Eine Ausstellung des Finnischen Glasmuseums Riihimäki Finnland 1998. Edited by Uta Laurén. Hämeenlinna, 1998.

Nuutajärvi. 200 vuotta suomalaista lasia. (200 years of Finnish glass). Published by Hackman Ltd. Edited by Tuula Poutasuo. Tampere, 1993.

Räsänen, Liisa, Kaj Franck: Muotoilijan tunnustuksia. (Confessions of a designer). *Form och miljö.* A series of the University of Art and Design B 12. Helsinki, 1989.

Timo Sarpaneva. Publication number 40 of the Helsinki City Museum, Helsinki, 1993.

Timo Sarpaneva: A retrospective. American Craft Museum, from March 17 to June 18, 1994. Published by the Helsinki City Museum of Art. Helsinki, 1994.

Suhonen, Pekka: R*espect for Man and Nature. Tapio Wirkkala and his Work.* Exposition catalogue. The Finnish Society of Crafts and Design. Helsinki, 1981.

Tapio Wirkkala Venini. Exposition catalogue of the Museum of Finnish Glas. Riihimäki, 1987.

Untracht, Oppi: *Saara Hopea-Untracht. Elämä ja työ. Life and Work.* Porvoo-Helsinki-Juva, 1988.

Seeking Beauty – Utility Objects in Finland

Ekholm, Kurt: Finland. *Form* 1/1948.

Ekholm, Kurt: Konstnärer i industrien. *Form* 2/1946.

Franck, Kaj: *Esitelmien muistiinpanoja* (Lecture notes). Nagoya 1956, University of Art and Design, 1976.

Franck, Kaj: Kauneutta etsimässä. *Kaunis Koti* 3/1949.

Gullichsen, Maire: Brukskonst i villovägar. *Hufvudstadsbladet* 1.10.1947.

Hald, Arthur: Kategorisk katalog. *Form* 1/1951.

Hald, Arthur: Servisen (Arabias styvbarn?) *Form* 1/1948.

Hald, Arthur: Väestöliittos vardagsvaror. *Form* 1/1948.

Johansson, Gotthard: Finlands bruksvara. *Svenska Dagbladet* 26.2.1954.

Kurkistamme astiakaappiin. *Keramiikka ja Lasi* 1/1956.

Saaritsa, Pentti: Menin sen verran sekaisin. From the collection *En osaa seisahtaa* 1969.

Stavenow, Åke: Arabia. En utställning på NK som manifesterar finsk kvalitet och konstkultur. *Form* 10/1945.

Modern Fashion Design in Finland

Form Function Finland 3–4/1997, 1–2, 4/1998.

Lappalainen, Piippa & Almay, Mirja : *Kansakunnan vaatettajat.* WSOY, Porvoo, 1996.

Muotisorja 1/1969.

Suhonen, Pekka & Pallasmaa, Juhani (eds.) : *Marimekkoilmiö (The Marimekko phenomenon)* Marimekko Oy. Espoo, 1986.

From Weave to Fibre

Forss, Maija & Priha, Päikki & Rantanen, Kirsti & Ylinen, Suvi: *Kankaanpainanta.* Espoo, 1979.

Kruskopf, Erik: Taidetekstiilin asema ja arvostus. *Arkkitehti* 1/77.

Priha, Päikki: *Pyhä kaunistus – Kirkkotekstiilit Suomen Käsityön Ystävien toiminnassa*

1904–1950. Taideteollinen korkeakoulu A 11. Jyväskylä, 1991.

Priha, Päikki: *Suomalaisen kirkkotekstiilien eläintarhat ja kukkivat puutarhat. Käytännöllinen teologia ja kirkko.* A book in honour *of* Pentti Lempiäinen for his 50th birthday Sept. 18th, 1992. Helsinki, 1992.

Priha, Päikki: *Suomalaisen tekstiilitaiteen vaiheita 1900-luvulla. Tekstiilitaiteilijat Texo 25,* 1956–1981. Forssa, 1981.

Rantanen, Kirsti: *Karvalangasta mattoa ennen.* Hämeen kirjapaino Oy, 1986.

Sata vuotta. Suomen Käsityön Ystävät 1879–1979 (A hundred years. Friends of the Finnish Handicraft 1879–1979). Exhibition catalogue, 1979.

Toikka-Karvonen, Annikki: Onko taidetekstiileillä sijaa? *Kaunis koti* 8/1971.

Vuorinen, Hilkka: Tekstiilit julkisessa tiloissa. *Kotiteollisuus* 2/1984.

A Story of Modern Finnish Furniture

Korvenmaa, Pekka: *Ilmari Tapiovaara. Design Classics.* Santa & Cole, Barcelona, 1997.

Sarantola-Weiss, Minna: *Kalusteita kaikille – Suomen puusepänteollisuuden historia.*

Puusepänteollisuuden liitto, Helsinki, 1995.

Schildt, Göran: *Alvar Aalto in his own Words.* Otava and Rizzoli, Keuruu, 1997.

Pekka Suhonen: *Artek – alku, tausta, kehitys,* 1985.

Index of names